# Linguistic Diversity in the South

# Linguistic Diversity in the South

*Changing Codes, Practices, and Ideology*

Edited by Margaret Bender

Southern Anthropological Society Proceedings, No. 37
Christopher P. Toumey, Executive Editor

The University of Georgia Press
*Athens & London*

Southern Anthropological Society
*Founded 1966*



Published by the University of Georgia Press
Athens, Georgia 30602


Printed and bound by Integrated Book Technology, Inc.
Printed in the United States of America

08 07 06 05 04 C 5 4 3 2 1
08 07 06 05 04 P 5 4 3 2 1

Library of Congress Cataloging-in-Publication Data

Linguistic diversity in the South : changing codes, practices, and ideology / edited by Margaret Bender.
p. cm. — (Southern Anthropological Society proceedings ; no. 37)
ISBN 0-8203-2585-6 (hardcover : alk. paper) —
ISBN 0-8203-2586-4 (pbk. : alk. paper)
1. English language—Southern States. 2. English language—Variation—Southern States. 3. English language—Dialects—Southern States. 4. Languages in contact—Southern States. 5. Americanisms—Southern States. 6. Southern States—Languages. I. Bender, Margaret Clelland. II. Series.
PE2922.L56 2004
427'.975—dc22 2004001446

British Library Cataloging-in-Publication Data available

# Contents

# Acknowledgments

Our thanks go to the 2000–2001 officers of the Southern Anthropological Society, who offered us the opportunity to hold the key symposium that produced this volume at the 2002 annual meeting of the SAS. We are also indebted to the sponsors of that conference: the Eastern Band of Cherokee Indians, the University of North Carolina at Asheville, Wake Forest University, and Western Carolina University.

# Linguistic Diversity in the South

# Introduction: Power and Belief in Southern Language

*Margaret Bender*

This volume grew out of a very exciting key symposium at the 2002 meeting of the Southern Anthropological Society. A diverse group of linguists and anthropologists working on language use in the South came together to present challenging new work that explores relationships among language, culture, and society in a wide variety of contexts and from an even wider variety of perspectives. Because the contributors to this symposium and volume include speakers of various Southern languages and dialects, we embody, rather than just report on, linguistic diversity. Susan Stans and Louise Gopher, with their firsthand report on the design and initial implementation of a Seminole language education project in Florida, add a welcome perspective to what might otherwise be a fairly typical, stylistically homogeneous collection of papers coming out of a discursive economy that, as Anita Puckett describes in this volume, presupposes an exclusive link between a specific academic discourse style and "truth," "knowledge," and "value." Their work, along with Walt Wolfram's on Ocracoke and Lumbee dialect awareness programs, shows the importance of the relationship between speaker/community member perspectives and scholarly perspectives on language use. These chapters also speak to the always present, but sometimes latent, relationship between linguistic scholarship and language advocacy that provided a backdrop for our symposium.

Most of the authors in this volume are not just describing but actively working in language maintenance or linguistic heritage or pride movements, and each chapter contributes to a better understanding of a speech community's complex heritage and affirms the richness of the group's cultural and linguistic identity. At a more general level, these chapters reflect the best that the human sciences have to offer: scholarly work that, through its careful presentation and analysis of data, combats bigotry, promotes enlightenment, and accentuates, rather than detracts from, the dignity of the human subjects whose lives and practices it describes. In his paper, Wolfram describes some of the ethical responsibilities and complications that are an inherent part of this sort of work—the power hierarchy that may exist within the community or between researchers and community members, the problems that arise when researchers promote an interest in the language that may not be there, the commodification of language that is often a part of linguistic or cultural revitalization, and so forth. And certainly the importance of those issues has been confirmed by many of the papers in this volume, which show that thinking about these issues has become a central part of doing sensitive and responsible research. Wolfram challenges us all to "actively pursue positive ways [to] return linguistic favors" to the communities in which we work. Several of this volume's authors take Wolfram's message to heart, though we are all growing in our ability to fully carry out his challenge.

This book is not, and makes no pretense of being, a comprehensive or even representative volume on southern linguistic diversity. The rich diversity of papers herein only hints at the incredible diversity of language and language use in the South—a diversity of which the general educated public outside of the South and outside of the world of language scholarship often seems to be unaware. An important area for future research in the South, for example, will be the impact of the greatly increasing immigration of Spanish-speaking people; we only touch on this issue briefly in Blair Rudes's helpful overview of the history of linguistic diversity in the Carolinas. On other important topics that we do not address directly, we nevertheless offer important food for thought. Several of the papers raise intriguing questions about gender complexity in patterns of language use and discourse styles, for example. Puckett shows how authoritative forms of discourse (academic and religious) contribute to the production of contemporary Melungeon and Scotch-Irish identities in Appalachia. Traditionally masculine, these discursive genres are indeed performed by men in her examples. Women, at least in the Scotch-Irish case, provide responsive personal narratives. The interaction between these discursive forms creates the essential relationship between the validating external discourses and the experiences of specific Appalachian individuals who assert their Melungeon or Scotch-Irish identities. Pamela Innes describes a primarily male linguistic genre, the performance of Muskogee (Creek) medicine-making language in Oklahoma, and acknowledges the limits her identity as a young woman place on her access to the linguistic details of this genre. In Shana Walton's discussion of Cajun

English, the most exaggerated examples of speech and behavior given by her consultants as at the extreme end of Cajun come from female speakers. Whether this pattern is more generally representative of the mobilization of Cajun speech would have to be determined by further study, but the question is intriguing.

We also do not directly address the orthographic diversity of the South, but our work raises questions for future exploration in this area. Kirk Hazen and Ellen Fluharty's work on Appalachian English(es) includes a discussion of the role of eye dialect in the perpetuation of the stereotype they call "Appalachian Drawl." One wonders what impact the written materials produced by dialect awareness projects of the kind discussed by Wolfram, and the orthographies used in them, will have on the relevant speech communities' ideologies of literacy, their own sense of the nature of their dialects, and outsiders' perception of their dialects. For the Native American languages discussed in this volume, orthographic issues may be particularly sensitive and important: In some Native American communities, there has been resistance to writing the traditional language; orthographic choice can affect pronunciation in communities with declining speakers; and controversies can sometimes arise over which orthography is best to use (e.g., see Walker 1984; Leap 1991; and Bender 2002a).

## DIVERSE PERSPECTIVES, DIVERSE LANGUAGES

Montgomery (1997:5) has pointed out that "far more has been written about Southern English than [about] any other variety or collections of varieties of American English." This observation appeared in an excellent and wide-ranging edited volume on Southern language variety (Bernstein, Nunnaly, and Sabino 1997) that itself augmented an already substantial body of resources on Southern speech. What we contribute to this wealth of material is a collection of papers that is balanced in its representation of anthropological and linguistic perspectives and that brings together case studies that are not routinely included in the same volume. Our discussions touch not only on Southern varieties of English (including Cajun English, which may not have received as much attention as other varieties [Eble 1993]) but on other languages as well. This collection reflects the patterns of immigration and settlement that have been so important to the shaping of Southern linguistic and cultural diversity. Particularly welcome to the ongoing scholarly discussion of Southern linguistic diversity, I believe, is our inclusion of two Native

American language cases and one example of Native American English (Innes's documentation of changing patterns of language use in Mvskoke, Stans and Gopher's outline of efforts to maintain the Creek and Mikasuki languages in Florida, and Wolfram's description of a Lumbee dialect awareness program). Our discussion of these languages and this dialect, together with the overview from Rudes, makes an obvious but important point about linguistic diversity that is sometimes glossed over: All speakers of European languages are immigrants to the South. A Cherokee acquaintance once told me a pointed story along these lines about being in a classroom setting with primarily non-Indians. The instructor asked if anyone in the class spoke a foreign language. Chuckling at the memory, she described how she had raised her hand and said, "Yes—English!" As Rudes points out, the South was linguistically diverse even prior to European contact. Some millennia ago, the Cherokees themselves may have migrated to the South, perhaps having separated from their Iroquoian cousins as recently as thirty-five hundred years ago (Scancarelli 1987:10).

Our diverse perspectives also allow us to explore linguistic variation and its relationship to society and culture at multiple levels. Some authors focus on the distribution of linguistic variables and how patterns of distribution may or may not map onto social and linguistic identities. Hazen and Fluharty, for example, consider the stereotyped and genuine features of Appalachian English and speakers' attitudes toward these; Christine Mallinson looks at the interplay between variables associated with African American speech and with Appalachian speech in a small, relatively isolated Appalachian community that includes both African Americans and European Americans.

Some of the authors explore the nature and range of linguistic codes. Rudes, for example, documents the numerous and changing codes that have been used in the Carolinas. Hazen and Fluharty, Mallinson, and Wolfram all touch on the value assigned to and the changing manifestations of specific codes—Appalachian English, African American English, Ocracoke English, and Lumbee English. Innes explores an apparent weakening of the link between the Mvskoke language as code and the ritual medicine performed at stompgrounds (traditional ceremonial grounds). As she describes, for some members of the Muskogee community, English is becoming acceptable as a substitute code in these religious contexts, which has implications for the meaning and range of use of both codes, Mvskoke and English.

In recent years, scholars have pointed out the increasing importance of the study of "discourse-level features" of Southern speech (Johnstone

1992:2–3; see also Bailey 1997:30–31). Innes, Puckett, and Walton add to the scholarly push in this direction while making it clear that Southern discourse, like Southern language, is a highly variable entity. Innes's example, in fact, pushes at the boundary of what Southernness means. If the South is a geographical area, and if that area is sometimes taken to include Oklahoma, then it seems reasonable to suggest that Mvskoke medicine-making language is a Southern discourse genre. This argument may also be supported by the fact that Mvskoke is now alternating with some variety of Southern English in the verbal repertoire of Muskogees, even in the most traditional of sociolinguistic contexts. What Innes documents is a shift in which the use of a specific code (Mvskoke) may no longer function as an exclusive index (sign via association) of a particular group identity (Muskogee medicine man), leading us to wonder how the presence or absence of that code at stompgrounds may begin to characterize the grounds and their ritual activities.

Several of our authors document the wide variety of ways in which linguistic performance and discourse relate to the expression, or indeed to the production, of specific ethnicities or other language-dependent identities. Walton, for example, explores how Cajun storytellers creatively use Cajun English to precisely position themselves as just Cajun enough to be proud, but not enough to be the object of ridicule. Puckett studies the discourses mobilized by members of Melungeon and Appalachian Scotch-Irish communities to validate their groups' ontological status and their own individual places in those groups.

Puckett's chapter takes us in an especially exciting direction with its treatment of the iconic relationship between (i.e., the meaning carried through the resemblance between) Melungeon identify-affirming discourse and both academic and religious discourse. How might other forms of discourse in the South be validated or otherwise made meaningful via the echoes or iconic appropriations they contain of other discourses? If the accepted code of Muskogee medicine-making language continues to shift toward English, for example, will English-language discourses provide the model for the new medicine-making language? Will the texts and other linguistic materials produced by the language and dialect awareness programs described by Wolfram provide iconic models for new programs in other communities?

The extensive ramifications of contact among languages and language varieties in the South merit ongoing study (Bailey 1997:28). We touch on some important cases of contact in this volume: the impact of English on Mvskoke/Creek and Mikasuki, the constitutive role of academic and religious discourse in the language of the Melungeon heritage movement, the effect of immersion in Standard American English and/or Southern English on speakers of Cajun, Appalachian, and Lumbee English. Mallinson provides an interesting complement with the questions she raises about the assimilative effect of rural isolation on the speech of the youngest African Americans in her Beech Bottom sample.

Montgomery (1996) posed the question of dialectal relativity: Do some varieties of English, he asked, exploring as examples the presence of multiple modals and the pronoun 'y'all' in Southern English, allow for grammatical-semantic distinctions that others do not? While none of our studies really follows this line of inquiry, we do move along a parallel one: Are there particular relationships among specific codes and/or linguistic genres on the one hand and specific cultural identities and their expressions on the other? Can one be Cajun in another dialect? Is the degree of Cajunness, understood in part as a cultural distance from the mainstream, indexed by the linguistic distance of one's Cajun speech from Standard English, as seems to be suggested by Walton's informants? Is the emerging Melungeon group identity Puckett explores expressible only through the sanctifying and legitimizing medium of academic-like discourse? Is the maintenance of Seminole and Miccosukee culture and identity inextricably linked to the maintenance of the Creek and Mikasuki languages? Innes shows how complex the answers to such questions can be when she demonstrates that the Mvskoke-speaking community with which she works is divided over the issue of whether traditional medicine can be legitimately performed in English rather than Mvskoke. The "social power of the indexicality of language" to "constitute reality not by naming and pointing to a preexisting object but by inverting the order of the indexed and indexing as if the indexed preceded the indexing" (Inoue 2002:412) is clearly integral to these relationships between language and cultural identities. The Melungeon and Scotch-Irish communities Puckett describes, for example, are being characterized anew daily by the circulation of their respective ethnonyms in the context of powerful discourse genres.

## IDEOLOGY AND CONSCIOUSNESS

One of the most important discussions to which we contribute is in the complex and intriguing area of language ideology. The study of language (or linguistic) ideology, defined by Silverstein (1979:193) as "any set of beliefs about language articulated by the users as a rationalization or justification of perceived language structure and use," has illuminated our understanding of how language works, why it changes, and in general, how linguistic detail is related to social institutions, practices, and meanings (e.g., see Woolard and Schieffelin 1994; Schieffelin, Woolard, and Kroskrity 1998). It has been especially informative to consider the triadic relations among linguistic ideology, language structure, and language use (Silverstein 1979; Hanks 1996) and how these then relate to questions of identity. Several of the studies presented in this volume teach us about such relationships.

Innes's work on Mvskoke presents a case of linguistic ideology shifting to match the fit between linguistic practice and social structure. That is, as English-speaking young men are replacing Mvskoke-speaking ones, a formerly held belief in the unique and inextricable link between Mvskoke and medicine is shifting for some community members. In other cases, linguistic practices reflect a shift in sociolinguistic ideology: For example, in Hazen and Fluharty's chapter and in Walton's, Appalachian and Cajun English speakers mock "extreme" members of their own speech communities, reflecting the reconfiguration of an external absolute value hierarchy in which Standard English is more valuable than either of these dialects into an internal value *scale* in which a "milder" form of the dialect is more valuable than a "stronger" one. In Hazen and Fluharty's examination of the linguistic markers present in stereotyped "Appalachian Drawl," those actually evident in particular varieties of Appalachian speech, and speakers' attitudes toward both, we see an excellent example of two necessary levels of this type of analysis—the study of ideology and the study of linguistic variability—informing each other quite productively.

Language ideology's enormous power is apparent in several chapters in this volume. It can contribute to social discrimination, as against Appalachian, Cajun, and Lumbee English speakers. At the other extreme, it can affirm identity, holding up language as evidence in support of a group's identity, worth, and very existence. Language ideology has recently played this role for some Native American groups in the South and elsewhere. Many Eastern Cherokees in North Carolina, for example, are extremely proud of and protective of their language as one marker of their tribe's genuine Native American status (Bender 2002b).

Just as language ideology can spur important social action, language ideologies are in turn powerfully affected by social forces. Innes shows how a language ideology is affected by the demographic shift of a declining speech community. Walton demonstrates that a shift in the economic value of group membership can affect attitudes toward dialect—in this case an increasingly positive attitude toward Cajun dialect. And Puckett depicts how the transformation of an ethnonym into a source of symbolic capital affects the discourse strategies and practices of the Melungeon identity movement.

We deal here not only with relationships between language ideology and language use, and language ideology and language structure, in a general sense. Several of these chapters deal with the specific issues related to the role language ideologies play in language *programs* and *movements*. While conscious and articulable beliefs about language always affect and are affected by language use, such beliefs are particularly foregrounded in language programs. Language programs, including language maintenance efforts, formal language education, and the kinds of linguistic pride movements that are sometimes linked with organized assertions of a group's cultural heritage, necessarily include linguistic ideologies, such as

> a belief that a specific language or dialect is inherently valuable and should be preserved, as is expressed in the Seminole case;
>
> a belief that language and linguistic diversity in general are valuable resources that should be preserved (a linguistic ideology that often shapes the actions of linguists and anthropologists, as Wolfram discusses);
>
> specific beliefs, about language in general or about a particular language or dialect, that direct the shape of a language program (for example, my own observation of the belief that Cherokee's structural differences from European languages make language education models derived from other languages useless);
>
> a kind of general Whorfianism that posits a language-culture link that is part of the justification for a language program, connecting the language to "cultural identity" (for example, the Mvskoke/Creek and Mikasuki languages have been associated with each group's identity and existence, though, interestingly, for Ocracoke and Cajun English speakers, language is more likely to be associated with the group's identity by outsiders than by community members);
>
> a belief that a specific language or dialect is uniquely appropriate to specific culturally significant linguistic genres or social contexts, which may be part of the explicit justification for a language program.

Although her chapter in this volume is not about Mvskoke language programs, Innes describes a case in which this last type of belief about Mvskoke—that it is uniquely suited for medicinal speech at stompgrounds—is shifting. Such shifts can erode the motivation for, or at least change the content of, language programs.

Language use more generally, however, though always affected by language ideology, does not necessarily involve this kind of foregrounding or conscious assertion of language ideology. In fact, speakers' unarticulated presuppositions about language often are of most interest. Perhaps even more interesting are the other, nonlinguistic, unarticulated cultural presuppositions that find their overt expression in language ideology. The Appalachian English speakers in Hazen and Fluharty's study who reject their own dialect or who struggle against peer pressure when they try to change dialects are grappling with fundamentally *social* conflicts that find their expression through discussions of language.

Speakers' levels of awareness of their presuppositions concerning language vary a great deal in our volume. In Puckett's chapter, we see speakers taking for granted the belief that ethnonyms have the power to confer socioeconomic and/or symbolic value on named or marked objects or practices; and this belief is connected to a belief that these groups and membership in them have inherent socioeconomic and/or symbolic value. In Stans and Gopher's chapter, the argument is clearly articulated that Seminole and Mikasuki have inherent value and should be maintained.

## OUTSIDER AND INSIDER LINGUISTIC IDEOLOGIES

Insider and outsider linguistic ideologies relate in a number of interesting ways, particularly where language programs and movements are concerned. Language education and preservation grants almost always involve the reconfiguration of a community's beliefs about language into ones comprehensible by funding agencies—for example, although a community may value its language or dialect for its own sake, a funding source may wish to see evidence of links between the maintenance of linguistic diversity and the general social or economic well-being of the community. Tourists (whose attention is sometimes drawn to dialectal difference by a community's dialect awareness programs, as Wolfram describes) may wish to see the most extreme representation of a local dialect, including eye dialect, whereas local community language ideology may dismiss or disparage the same usages. Puckett shows how an external linguistic ideology that grants transparency and authority to academic language then supports a local cultural ideology recognizing Melungeons as "white," through the circulation of the ethnonym 'Melungeon' in language that self-consciously indexes "one of the highest forms of whiteness." Interestingly, if the very same scholars who are providing the discursive model for this community do not uphold this linkage, their criticism is rejected because, say the community members, "Melungeon is ours." What was originally an exonym becomes an ethnonym, and defiantly so. Walton shows that "the way one talks" is seen as a litmus test for Cajun identity as determined by outsiders, but not the primary mode of defining Cajun identity by insiders; Wolfram reports a similar situation in the Ocracoke community, probably manifested in its most extreme version by the consultant who said, "The only person who worries about the dialect is Walt Wolfram." Innes depicts how a belief in the economic value of English (coming presumably in part from the dominant society) affects the value of Mvskoke in a relational way; Mvskoke is now seen as having a deficit in that regard.

One of the insider-outsider ideological gaps that can be the hardest to deal with is the one that sometimes exists on the topic of the inherent value of linguistic diversity, between linguists and linguistic anthropologists on the one hand and members of the communities in which they work on the other. Linguist Peter Ladefoged (1992) chided his peers for assuming that the value they assign to all languages and dialects is universally shared. Speech communities should set their own priorities, he has argued, in terms of language maintenance, revitalization, or assimilation. In general, as Ladefoged suggests, linguists and anthropologists are probably among those most likely to believe that linguistic diversity is inherently valuable and that efforts should be made to preserve threatened languages and dialects. But we see evidence of other points of view in this book. The assimilative linguistic melting pot of the United States provides the backdrop to Rudes's account of how English gained and more recently lost its monolithic status in the Carolinas. Wolfram relates that some Ocracoke English speakers find his concern for the dialect odd, and that some Lumbees are even offended by the attention his work calls to Lumbee English and its differences from Standard English. In general, Wolfram attributes the latter phenomenon to the "principle of linguistic inferiority," according to which "the speech of socially subordinate groups will be interpreted as linguistically deficient by comparison with socially dominant groups." Innes depicts a shift in language ideology that perhaps reflects a resigned coming to terms with a pending language shift from Mvskoke to English, whereas Stans and Gopher depict a strong and overt resistance to language shift that parallels the proactive linguist-activist stance.

There are also less positive outsider perspectives on language variety, of course. The stereotypes against which speakers struggle do not come from nowhere. Hazen and Fluharty show that stereotypes about Appalachian dialect, while they do not match reality, may affect community members' attitudes toward their own speech, causing them to self-consciously reject certain markers, such as 'y'all.' Walton shows how Cajun English speakers reappropriate and mobilize an external stereotype about Cajuns and their speech to position themselves very precisely within Cajun ethnic identity. Some speakers effectively distance themselves from the stereotypes associated with their cultural group by performing a kind of linguistic caricature.

## CULTURAL REPRODUCTION AND LANGUAGE SHIFT

Something that is sometimes less than obvious when we set our scholarly focus on language shift or language loss is that there are culturally specific ways of using language (and hence, forms of social action) that do not require the speaking of a group's traditional language or dialect (see, for example, Jaffe 1999 and Bender 2002a). Innes expresses concern over the shifting relative values of Mvskoke and English in medicine-making language; this concern is understandable and perhaps echoes that shared by many Mvskoke speakers. However, language shift does not always mean the loss of all of the grammatical and lexical classifications, and especially not of the linguistic practices, that contribute to a group's assertion and reproduction of itself as a living body. We need to keep our eyes open for these kinds of linguistic and cultural changes that are simultaneous perpetuations and transformations.

As language shift occurs, we need to consider what kinds of new divisions of linguistic labor emerge, and with what concomitant ideological justifications. In the Mvskoke case, will there be certain types of medicine that can be practiced only using Mvskoke while other types may be enacted through English? What kinds of differences will emerge between fluent Mvskoke-speaking medicine men and the grounds with which they are associated and nonfluent speakers and their respective grounds? Will the linguistic ideology linking Mvskoke and medicine affect the cultural value of medicine, or will the linguistic ideology shift? We see a hint of a shift in ideology when Innes tells us that for some Muskogee community members, the belief that fluency is a prerequisite for efficacious medicine is being replaced by a belief that rote memorization and repetition of chants and songs is sufficient—a fairly radical shift in how the relationship between the medicine man and the receiver of his message is understood.

Along similar lines, one wonders what will happen with Creek as it moves into the classroom. Children learning Creek and Mikasuki through the formal educational pullout program described by Stans and Gopher are not participants in the same process of language socialization as their elders. Therefore, from the point of view of language in use, they will not be learning the *same* Creek. (For examples of the impact of language socialization on language use, see Schieffelin and Ochs 1986 and Schieffelin 1990.) The meaning and function of formal education will also change in the lives of the participating students. Rampton (2002) has recently shown how students can appropriate the ritualistic processes of formal language education and mobilize elements of them in verbal play in other contexts. One can only wonder how the uses of Creek and Mikasuki in these classrooms will spill over in creative ways into other aspects of children's lives, in their interactions with speakers and with nonspeakers. Elsewhere (Bender 2002b) I describe an experience I had in a community library in which Cherokee language students used their new Cherokee literacy skills to pass notes in front of me. The objective of this activity was probably not to exclude me, since the students observed me also studying the Cherokee writing system at another table in the library. Neither was it to protectively encode their messages, since the children went out of their way to make their efforts visible to me. They were clearly engaged in a highly creative act of communicative play, perhaps designed to include me but at the same time to assert themselves as Cherokee in a way that did not include me. How might the Seminole language students in the pullout program begin using their language skills? Will they become a special group indexically marked by their ability to speak Creek? Will they begin to take on specialized social functions?

These kinds of questions are also important to ask about English dialects, including the ones explored in this book. As dialect awareness grows, through targeted programs, tourism, and other means, in what new ways will these dialects be mobilized and what new language ideologies will emerge? What specific discourse genres or linguistic forms will emerge in the changing contexts provided by tourism and language programs? How will the inevitable change in these dialects be related to the equally inevitable changes in these identities: O'cocker, Lumbee, Appalachian, African American, Cajun, Melungeon?

## REFERENCES


Bailey, Guy. 1997. Southern American English: A Prospective. In *Language Variety in the South Revisited,* ed. C. Bernstein, Thomas Nunnaly, and Robin Sabino, pp. 21–31. Tuscaloosa: University of Alabama Press.

Bender, Margaret. 2002a. From "Easy Phonetics" to the Syllabary: An Orthographic Division of Labor in Cherokee Language Education. *Anthropology and Education Quarterly* 33(1):90–117.

———. 2002b. *Signs of Cherokee Culture: Sequoyah's Syllabary in Eastern Cherokee Life*. Chapel Hill: University of North Carolina Press.

Bernstein, Cynthia, Thomas Nunnaly, and Robin Sabino, eds. 1997. *Language Variety in the South Revisited*. Tuscaloosa: University of Alabama Press.

Desjarlais, Robert. 1996. The Office of Reason: On the Politics of Language and Agency in a Shelter for "the Homeless Mentally Ill." *American Ethnologist* 23(4):880–900.

Eble, Connie. 1993. Prolegomenon to the Study of Cajun English. *SECOL Review* 17(2):165–177.

Hanks, William F. 1996. *Language and Communicative Practices*. Boulder: Westview.

Inoue, Miyako. 2002. Gender, Language, and Modernity: Toward an Effective History of Japanese Women's Language. *American Ethnologist* 29(2):392–422.

Jaffe, Alexandra. 1999. *Ideologies in Action: Language Politics on Corsica*. Berlin: Mouton de Gruyter.

Johnstone, Barbara. 1992. Violence and Civility in Discourse: Uses of Mitigation by Rural Southern White Men. *SECOL Review* 16(1):1–19.

Ladefoged, Peter. 1992. Another View of Endangered Languages. *Language* 68: 809–811.

Leap, William L. 1991. Pathways and Barriers to Indian Language Literacy-Building on the Northern Ute Reservation. *Anthropology and Education Quarterly* 22:21–41.

Montgomery, Michael. 1996. The Future of Southern American English. *SECOL Review* 20(1):1–24.

———. 1997. Language Variety in the South: A Retrospective and Assessment. In *Language Variety in the South Revisited,* ed. C. Bernstein, Thomas Nunnaly, and Robin Sabino, pp. 3–20. Tuscaloosa: University of Alabama Press.

Rampton, Ben. 2002. Ritual and Foreign Language Practices at School. *Language in Society* 31:491–525.

Scancarelli, Janine. 1987. *Grammatical Relations and Verb Agreement in Cherokee.* Ph.D. dissertation, University of California, Los Angeles.

Schieffelin, Bambi B. 1990. *The Give and Take of Everyday Life: Language Socialization of Kaluli Children.* Cambridge: Cambridge University Press.

Schieffelin, Bambi B., and Elinor Ochs, eds. 1986. *Language Socialization across Cultures.* Cambridge: Cambridge University Press.

Schieffelin, Bambi B., Kathryn A. Woolard, and Paul V. Kroskrity, eds. 1998. *Language Ideologies: Practice and Theory.* Oxford: Oxford University Press.

Silverstein, Michael. 1979. Language Structure and Linguistic Ideology. In *The Elements: A Parasession on Linguistic Units and Levels,* ed. Paul R. Clyne, William F. Hanks, and Carol L. Hofbauer, pp. 193–247. Chicago: Chicago Linguistic Society.

Walker, Willard. 1984. Literacy, Wampums, the gúdəbuk, and How Indians in the Far Northeast Read. *Anthropological Linguistics* 26(1):42–52.

Woolard, Kathryn A., and Bambi B. Schieffelin. 1994. Language Ideology. *Annual Review of Anthropology* 23:55–82.

# Dialect Awareness in Community Perspective

*Walt Wolfram*

Sociolinguists, like many other social science researchers, often feel a sense of indebtedness and obligation to the subjects who provide data for their research and the communities where they carry out their fieldwork. Even the most limited field-initiated study entails a relationship with a network of speakers, and many sociolinguists spend extended periods of time as participant observers in the speech communities where they conduct their research. The nature of the relationship between researchers and the people they study has become an increasing matter of concern for researchers, for professional organizations, and, in some instances, for the host communities. In what ways, and to what extent, are researchers obligated to the communities they study? How might communities help define the parameters of research and preserve their rights during and after the research? Is it possible to establish researcher-researched partnerships that are mutually responsible and beneficial? How can researchers give back to communities as they collect data driven by fundamental research questions? These are questions that face all responsible social science researchers who conduct research that involves human subjects.

These questions apply not only to sociolinguistics but also to the broad scope of linguistic description. As Rickford (1997:186) observes, "The unequal partnership between sociolinguistics and the . . . speech community . . . represents a far more general problem between linguistics and the community of speakers whose data fuel our descriptive grammars, theories, and careers." Although the relationship between researchers and host communities for research has always been an issue for studies involving human subjects, it is only beginning to receive the reflective scrutiny it deserves. Attention to such relationships now ranges from Institutional Review

Board approval, currently required for all government-sponsored research involving human subjects, to reflective discussions among researchers as to how they relate personally, socially, and professionally to the communities where they conduct their research (Cameron, Frazer, Harvey, Rampton, and Richardson 1992).

In this presentation, I consider the relationship between researchers and communities in the implementation of so-called dialect awareness programs. The term *dialect awareness program* is used here to refer to activities that are directed toward promoting an understanding of and appreciation for language variation. This type of program falls under the more general rubric of language awareness programs directed toward raising "a person's sensitivity to and conscious awareness of the nature of language and its role in human life" (Donmall 1985:7). Such programs may emphasize a cognitive parameter, in which the focus is on understanding the patterns of language; an affective parameter, in which the focus is on attitudes about language; or a social parameter, in which the focus is on the use of language in effective communication and interaction. In particular, I am concerned with the design of awareness programs that use research data from the communities themselves as a basis for establishing the program, though, of course, such programs may also be implemented as a general type of linguistic outreach activity apart from community-based research. In the following discussion, I first situate dialect awareness programs in terms of current principles of sociolinguistic involvement and the ethics of researcher-researched relationships. I then describe two specific programs that have been established in different communities of North Carolina, one on the island of Ocracoke, located on the Outer Banks of North Carolina, and one in Robeson County, located in the sand hills of southeastern North Carolina. Finally, I reflect on some of the social, ethical, and ideological issues attendant to these programs as they relate to the role of sociolinguists in public life (Heller, Rickford, Laforest, and Cyr 1999). If nothing else, a personal perspective can raise issues for further consideration by members of the academy as they reflect on their role in and their relationship to communities that provide data for their research.

## PRINCIPLES OF SOCIOLINGUISTIC INVOLVEMENT

The relatively short history of social dialectology has demonstrated that it is quite possible to combine a commitment to the description of sociolinguistic data and a concern for social issues relating to dialect diversity. According to Labov (1982:172–73), there are two primary principles that should motivate linguists to take social action, namely, the principle of error correction and the principle of debt incurred. These are stated as follows:

> PRINCIPLE OF ERROR CORRECTION
> A scientist who becomes aware of a widespread idea or social practice with important consequences that is invalidated by his [*sic*] own data is obligated to bring this error to the attention of the widest possible audience. . . .
>
> PRINCIPLE OF DEBT INCURRED
> An investigator who has obtained linguistic data from members of a speech community has an obligation to use the knowledge based on that data for the benefit of the community, when it has need of it.

Over the past several decades, there have been several exemplary cases where these principles have been applied. In the 1960s, sociolinguists in the United States took a strong pro-difference stance in the so-called deficit-difference controversy that was taking place within education in general and within speech and language pathology in particular (Baratz 1968; Labov 1970; Wolfram 1970). Consistent with the principle of error correction, sociolinguists took a united stand against the classification and treatment of natural dialect differences as language deficits or disorders. There is little doubt that sociolinguists played a major role in pushing the definition of linguistic normalcy toward a dialect-sensitive one, although the practical consequences of this definition are still being worked out in many clinical and educational settings (Wolfram, Adger, and Christian 1999).

In keeping with the principle of debt incurred, social dialectologists also rose to the occasion in a legal case referred to as the Ann Arbor Decision (1979). Linguistic testimony was critical to the judge's ruling in favor of the African American children who brought suit against the Ann Arbor, Michigan, Board of Education for not taking the children's dialect into account in reading instruction (Farr-Whiteman 1980). In effect, the judge ruled that the defendants had failed to take appropriate action to overcome language barriers in relation to the students' dialect. In compliance with the judge's ruling, a series of workshops was conducted to upgrade awareness about language variation and to demonstrate how to apply sociolinguistic expertise in reading instruction.

Linguists were also quite active in their support of the resolution by the Oakland Unified School District Board of Education in 1996 and 1997 affirming the legitimacy of African American Vernacular English as a language system. Linguists attempted to explain to the American public why such a resolution was appropriate and even testified on behalf of the Oakland School Board at a U.S. Senate subcommittee hearing on the status of this variety and its potential role in education. Some linguists have been quite active in combining their descriptions of language variation with a social commitment to apply their knowledge to language-related social and educational problems (e.g., Labov 1982; Rickford 1999; Baugh 2001).

There is another level of social commitment that sociolinguistic investigators might strive for in communities where they conduct their research. This level is more positive and proactive in that it involves the active pursuit of ways to return linguistic favors to the community. In Wolfram 1993 (227) I therefore proposed an additional principle of social commitment called the principle of linguistic gratuity.

> PRINCIPLE OF LINGUISTIC GRATUITY
> Investigators who have obtained linguistic data from members of a speech community should actively pursue positive ways in which they can return linguistic favors to the community.

Language-related activities under this principle may range from service to community organizations such as civic groups, museums, churches, and schools to the production of language-related materials and products on behalf of and with the community.

There are, of course, several different levels of relationships that may exist between researchers and research communities, as well as different kinds of roles that researchers may assume within communities (Briggs 1986). Cameron et al. (1992) delimit three primary kinds of relationships. In *ethical research,* the concern is to "minimize damage and offset inconvenience to the researched and to acknowledge their [i.e., community members'] contribution," but the underlying model is focused on "research *on*" social subjects (Cameron et al. 1992:14). This level of relationship ensures compliance with, but does not extend beyond, institutional guidelines assured under the Protection of Human Subject approval forms now required for most institutionally based research on human subjects. An *advocacy position* is characterized by a commitment on the part of the researcher "to do research *on* and *for* subjects" in such a way that the researcher's skills or "expert opinion" is used "to defend subjects' interests" (Cameron et al. 1992:15). Although terms such as "expert opinion" and "subjects' interests" are admittedly socially constructed, ideologically loaded notions that need to be scrutinized in detail, the goal of an advocacy program is distinguished from an ethical concern for the treatment of subjects and subjects' rights. The third level, *empowered research,* involves "research *on, for,* and *with*" the community (Cameron et al. 1992:22). This level of community involvement implies the use of interactive or dialogic research methods as opposed to the conventional objectifying strategies positivists apply in their research. In empowered research, subjects have their own agendas and the researcher-community relationship is shaped by a commitment to address these concerns as determined by the community.

Most dialect awareness programs fall under the linguistic gratuity principle in terms of sociolinguistic involvement and under the advocacy position in terms of the relationship of the researcher to the researched. They do not typically involve empowered research, though some aspects of dialect preservation and language revitalization programs may, in fact, derive from community-based concerns and requests. At the foundation of the kinds of programs discussed here is a concern for the flow of information that includes the community itself. As Cameron et al. (1992:24) note, "if information is worth having, it is worth sharing." Our dialect awareness programs with local communities are, in fact, motivated by a primary commitment to the notion that information about language variation should be shared with the community whose data has fueled our research.

## THE COMMUNITY CONTEXT OF DIALECT AWARENESS

Though sociolinguistic research is hardly restricted to a particular type of language community, the vast majority of our studies over the past several decades have centered on vernacular, or so-called nonmainstream, dialect communities (e.g., Wolfram 1969, 1974; Wolfram and Schilling-Estes 1995, 1997; Wolfram and Thomas 2002). This focus presents a special challenge for dialect awareness programs centered on language varieties that have been traditionally stigmatized. At the same time, however, it offers a unique opportunity to address issues of sociolinguistic inequality in terms of cognitive, affective, and social parameters. Dialects spoken by socially subordinate groups are invariably subject to the principle of linguistic inferiority (Wolfram and Schilling-Estes 1998:6), which maintains that the speech of socially subordinate groups will be interpreted as linguistically deficient by comparison with that of socially dominant groups. In most instances, vernacular dialect structures are viewed simply as unworthy approximations of Standard English—violations of proper grammar with no linguistic integrity in their own right. Speakers of socially favored varieties are not the only ones who embrace this belief; speakers of vernacular dialects themselves also hold it.

Communities that have been socialized into believing that their language variety is nothing more than "bad speech" are not particularly eager to celebrate what they view as linguistic inferiority. This lack of enthusiasm presents a significant obstacle for the development of dialect awareness programs. Even when a vernacular-speaking community has an appreciation for the usefulness of its indigenous dialect on a community-based, interactional level, such appreciation is usually coupled with at least an overt expression of linguistic inferiority. A goal of virtually all dialect awareness programs therefore is to apply the principle of error correction by replacing the popular mythology about language diversity with an understanding of the naturalness and legitimacy of language variation regardless of social valuation. Linguists bring to the community an understanding about language structure that is usually at odds with the broadly based linguistic ideology—in effect, a competing belief system about linguistic diversity. Admittedly, linguists are "ideological brokers" (Blommaert 1999:9) who bid to replace a prevailing, popular language ideology with an alternative view of language (Milroy 2001). Confronting negative linguistic self-images while working with dialect communities to preserve and appreciate local linguistic heritage is generally the most critical challenge confronting researcher-community partnerships in nonmainstream community settings. In fact, the inability to ameliorate this ideological conflict is the primary reason I have personally failed to develop dialect awareness programs in a number of communities where I have carried out research over the past several decades—and it continues to be the biggest single hurdle for implementing such programs.

In the following section, I outline two dialect awareness programs in quite different community settings, one on the remote Outer Banks island of Ocracoke, where a unique dialect is rapidly dissipating, and one in Robeson County, North Carolina, where a Native American Indian ethnic variety, though changing, remains quite robust. As set forth in Wolfram, Adger, and Christian 1999, the rationale for dialect awareness programs is based on humanistic, scientific, and sociohistorical foundations. From a humanistic perspective, such programs are meant to develop an appreciation for the naturalness of linguistic diversity in the context of multiculturalism; from a scientific perspective, they are designed to explicate the intricacy of linguistic patterning as a kind of scientific inquiry; and from a sociohistorical perspective, they are intended to probe the role of language and dialect in the historical and cultural development of a community. In describing the programs I use a comparative, case-study format. The two cases of programmatic implementation share certain features though they represent quite different sociohistorical and community contexts.

## DIALECT AWARENESS PROGRAMS IN PRACTICE

Both Ocracoke and the Lumbee Native American Indian community in Robeson County are historically isolated communities that have existed apart from more widely dispersed populations for quite different reasons. Ocracoke is a small, distinct community separated from the mainland by a twenty-mile stretch of the Pamlico Sound. Since the first decade of the eighteenth century it has been inhabited by European Americans, and, with the exception of one member of a longstanding African American family, it is now a monoethnic population. The community was originally established on the need to pilot cargo ships from the Atlantic Ocean through the shallow, shifting Ocracoke Inlet in their passage to the mainland. With changes in the shipping industry and the physical reshaping of barrier island inlets, however, the need for piloting became obsolete and the island turned to other marine-based forms of subsistence. Over the past half century Ocracoke has been transformed into a popular tourist site, and the economy has shifted to a service industry hosting up to six thousand daily visitors during the height of the summer tourist season. There are approximately seven hundred permanent residents on Ocracoke, half of whom are *O'cockers,* the local designation for families who can trace their island roots at least several generations, if not back to the eighteenth century. Over the centuries, island residents nurtured a unique dialect known as the Brogue or Hoi Toider Speech. With the flood of tourists and new residents from the mainland, however, this once-vibrant variety has been rapidly eroding. During the last decade, linguists from the North Carolina Language and Life Project have been describing change and variation in Ocracoke speech. Their descriptions are based on extensive sociolinguistic interviews with more than eighty lifetime residents ranging from ten to ninety-six years of age. Several books (e.g., Wolfram and Schilling-Estes 1997; Wolfram, Hazen, and Schilling-Estes 1999) and more than two dozen articles have been written on sociolinguistic research topics that extend from dialect death (Wolfram and

Schilling-Estes 1995) to "performance styles" of the traditional Ocracoke Brogue (Schilling-Estes 1998). At the same time, our research team has engaged in an extensive dialect awareness program, making it a good case study for examining researcher-community relations.

From the outset of our research on Ocracoke, we have actively engaged in a range of activities to inform the residents of the host community and the general public about the dialect heritage of the community. These involve both formal and informal educational activities with different types of community agencies that include the following:

> The establishment of a permanent exhibit on the Ocracoke Brogue for the museum operated by the Ocracoke Preservation Society (OPS). The exhibit includes panels on the history and development of the dialect, its current moribund status, and a list of some distinct lexical items. The centerpiece of the exhibit is a continuously playing documentary video, *The Ocracoke Brogue* (Blanton and Waters 1995). The exhibit was funded by a grant from the Outer Banks Foundation obtained by the research staff of the North Carolina Language and Life Project on behalf of the OPS.
>
> The production of a video documentary on the Ocracoke Brogue (Blanton and Waters 1995). In addition to its showing at the OPS, the documentary has been aired on local television in eastern North Carolina and shown in other informal and formal educational venues. It is distributed by the museum, with all revenues from its sale going to the OPS.
>
> The development of a weeklong middle-school dialect awareness curriculum on dialect diversity and the Ocracoke dialect, including a forty-two-page student text titled *Dialects and the Ocracoke Brogue* (Wolfram, Schilling-Estes, and Hazen 1995). The curriculum has been taught to eighth-grade students at the Ocracoke Public School since 1994.
>
> The publication of a book on the Ocracoke dialect for general audiences, titled *Hoi Toide on the Outer Banks: The Story of the Ocracoke Brogue* (Wolfram and Schilling-Estes 1997). The book is available at tourist sites on the island and in popular bookstores, lighthouses, and museums around the state. Half of all royalties from its sale go to the OPS.

The development and production a CD/cassette titled *Ocracoke Speaks*. This collection of stories and anecdotes from more than thirty speakers selected from our sociolinguistic interviews was compiled in collaboration with local historian Ellen Fulcher Cloud. A thousand copies were donated to the OPS, with all revenues from its sale going to the Ocracoke museum.

The design and distribution of a souvenir T-shirt with the slogan "Save the Brogue" printed on the front of the shirt and a set of unique dialect terms printed on the back. The shirt is distributed at the museum operated by the OPS, with all revenues from its sale donated to the OPS.

The presentation of a series of lectures and workshops on dialect variation and Outer Banks speech for community groups (e.g., the Back Porch series hosted by the OPS) and for Outer Banks visitors (e.g., visiting groups of students, teachers, and other groups).

Cooperation with the media to produce feature stories on the historical roots of the Ocracoke Brogue, its moribund state, and the dialect curriculum. Feature articles have appeared in newspapers ranging from the *London Times* to the local Ocracoke school newspaper; television and radio coverage has varied from a BBC-produced feature story aired on CNN International to local television and National Public Radio spots.

Although our sociolinguistic research in the Lumbee community in Robeson County is similar in some respects to that conducted on Ocracoke, the sociolinguistic issues are somewhat different and the community contexts are quite dissimilar. The primary sociolinguistic focus of our study of Lumbee English is language and ethnicity over time and place, as opposed to the focus on language change in Ocracoke. Differences in the two communities include ethnic composition, sociopolitical status, sociohistorical context, and community size. The Lumbee are the largest Native American community east of the Mississippi River, with more than fifty-four thousand members on the tribal rolls. Almost forty-seven thousand Lumbee live in Robeson County, North Carolina, where they comprise 38% of the population (33% is European American, 25% African American, and 4% other, including a growing Hispanic population). Although the Lumbee have a strong sense of Native American Indian identity that has existed for a couple of centuries and although they are fully recognized on the state level, their federal status as a Native American tribe remains ambiguous. They are recognized as Native American Indians (Congressional Act of 1956) but do not have entitlements such as reservation land or benefits from the Bureau of Indian Affairs. Furthermore, their language situation is quite different from that of the European Americans on Ocracoke. The Lumbee lost their Native American language generations ago, and the social and historical circumstances of the region have made it difficult to determine precisely what ancestral language or languages they may have spoken originally. At the same time, the Lumbee have developed a unique ethnolinguistic variety of English that is neither white nor black—a linguistic other in the triethnic context of Robeson County. Since 1993, the staff of the North Carolina Language and Life Project has been researching both objective and subjective dimensions of this ethnolinguistic variety, and two books (Dannenberg 2002; Wolfram, Dannenberg, Knick, and Oxendine 2002) and more than twenty research articles have been written on this topic. In addition, seven master's theses have been written on topics related to Lumbee English, including four by residents of Robeson County; two of these were written by members of the Lumbee community (Hammonds 2000; Kerns 2001).

We have also carried out several different types of dialect awareness programs in collaboration with the Lumbee community. Among these programs are the following:

> The establishment of a permanent exhibit on Lumbee English for the Museum of the Native American Resource Center in Pembroke, North Carolina. The exhibit features four panels, one highlighting the ancestral language situation of the Lumbee, one presenting the development of their unique Lumbee English dialect, one discussing dialect and identity, and one featuring distinctive lexical items of Lumbee English. The exhibit also includes an interactive, computerized program featuring a touch-screen monitor. The software allows visitors to select from a menu a variety of two-minute video vignettes that range from a presentation on the history of Lumbee English to an interactive vocabulary quiz on Lumbee English. The exhibit was funded by an Informal Science Education grant from the National Science Foundation.

> The production of a video documentary on Lumbee English titled *Indian by Birth: The Lumbee Dialect* (Hutcheson and Wolfram 2000). The documentary was aired on the North Carolina affiliate

of PBS and is distributed in video format by the Museum of the Native American Resource Center in Pembroke. All profits from its sale go to the museum.

The publication of a book, *Fine in the World: Lumbee Language in Time and Place,* written for a general audience (Wolfram et al. 2002), distributed through the museum and through the North Carolina State University Extension publications program. All proceeds from its sale in Pembroke go directly to the efforts of the museum. Two of the authors are from the Pembroke community; Stanley Knick is the director of the Museum of the Native American Resource Center and Linda Oxendine, a member of the Lumbee community, is director of the American Indian Studies Department at the University of North Carolina at Pembroke. The university was originally established in the 1880s as an Indian Normal School for the training of Native American teachers, but it has since become part of the University of North Carolina system.

Cooperation with a variety of journalists and other media specialists to produce feature stories on the historical roots and the current state of Lumbee English. Articles have appeared in local and regional newspapers and have been distributed nationally by the Associated Press. Television and radio coverage has ranged from airing feature stories on National Public Radio to airing video highlights and the documentary on the state PBS affiliate, WUNC-TV.

The presentation of workshops on Lumbee English for teachers in Robeson County and special presentations on language diversity and Lumbee English to elementary school students in Robeson County.

Although our activities in Robeson County have not been as extensive as those carried out in Ocracoke, they have engaged more local residents in their production. Together, the two efforts probably represent the most extensive community-based dialect awareness programs in the United States, and they have been featured as model programs at various professional meetings, as well as at conferences and meetings for state educators. At the same time, they raise a number of issues about the role of such programs in local communities and the nature of relationships between linguists and community residents in their implementation. In the subsequent discussion,

I probe some of these underlying issues. The focus is not on their relative "success" or "failure" per se, but on the kinds of relationships they represent between researchers and local residents.

## DECONSTRUCTING LINGUISTIC GRATUITY

Our attempts to return linguistic favors through dialect awareness programs have involved social, educational, and economical alliances.[1] Although I would like to think of our programs as a model of how sociolinguistic researchers might work productively with a community on language issues, I am aware that community-based dialect awareness programs and community-researcher partnerships raise deeper issues about the role of sociolinguistic researchers in local communities. In principle, probably few sociolinguists are opposed to giving back to host research communities and to establishing collaborative relationships with local communities in ways that might benefit them. But we also must recognize that notions such as "favors," "collaboration," and "benefit" are ideologically laden. Furthermore, working out the everyday details of gratuity and negotiating community-based partnerships can often be complicated and controversial, as these partnerships move toward general principles to guide researcher-community relations in the dialect awareness programs. I address several issues that are specific to the programs in Ocracoke and Robeson County, but from these case studies also emerge some ethical, sociopolitical, and ideological concerns that might apply to sociolinguistic partnerships in general.

One of the immediate issues that emerges in a researcher-community partnership involves relationships of power and authority. Although the members of a research team may assume a variety of situated roles and relationships with community members as visitors, researchers, and friends, our initial and primary status in these communities is framed by our status as university-based language experts. We have never attempted to disguise our role as researchers who study language variation. In presenting ourselves as the "dialect people" (a common reference by residents of the communities who don't know us personally), we have been assigned status as language authorities. In other domains of knowledge, such as the ways of the water on Ocracoke and cultural and historical knowledge of the Lumbee people, we may rightly be considered naive or ignorant, but when it comes to general matters of language variation we have been ascribed "expert status." This position carries with it an associated set of privileges and opportunities. In fact, we were provided the initial opportunity to develop our programs and activities because of this status. Acceptance on a personal level by the members of the indigenous communities does not rest on academic credentials or expert status. In fact, such status is more of an obstacle than an asset in establishing personal friendships: our specialized language expertise creates an asymmetrical authority relationship in matters of language.

The authority relationship in the language domain further affects issues of ownership with respect to language-related activities. Notwithstanding the fact that some community members have repeatedly indicated their appreciation for the programs and activities undertaken to celebrate the community dialect heritage, they are still thought of as "Walt Wolfram's programs," not the community's programs. In fact, one of the most telling statements about our programs came from a classroom teacher in Ocracoke who gave a glowing testimonial about the significance of dialect awareness program carried out in her class by noting that "the pride that has been established through Walt's program is phenomenal." I have also received several dozen e-mails from members of the Lumbee community who have thanked me for what we have done on behalf of the community's language heritage. As favorable as these comments seem, they still indicate that ownership of the programs is vested outside the community. Parenthetically, it might also be observed that the identification of the programs as "Walt's" further disregards the role of staff members who have done research quite independently and on occasion have challenged the findings of the most highly profiled member of the team, raising yet another issue of ownership with respect to the research domain within the academy.

The only domain of language where community members have claimed some proprietary language rights involves the lexicon. Not surprisingly, community residents in both Ocracoke and Robeson County have occasionally but symbolically challenged our definitions of "dialect words," and a few residents in these communities have even taken it upon themselves to collect sets of words and sayings on their own. On the other hand, no community member has yet challenged us about our morphosyntactic descriptions. I view the involvement of local residents in the collection and presentation of lexicons as a good sign, and in at least one case a local resident is the first author on a community-based lexicon (Locklear, Wolfram, Schilling-Estes, and Dannenberg 1999) because of his proactive involvement in the collection of lexical items. But we must also admit that, following discussion and consultation with these local dialect word collectors, we outsider researchers have typically presumed the right to make final decisions about the items to be included or excluded in the published dialect dictionary of island speech. For example, community collectors of lexical items do not necessarily know which items are locally restricted and which ones are more broadly distributed. Thus, there is limited empowerment even in terms of the community's role in the construction of a local dialect dictionary.

An incident over a museum exhibit constructed at one of the community sites illustrates how we have sometimes unwittingly preempted the partnership relationship. On behalf of the Ocracoke Preservation Society, we wrote a grant proposal to design and construct a permanent exhibit on the Ocracoke Brogue at the museum, complete with background paneling, photos, and bulleted statements highlighting the nature of the dialect. The exhibit was designed and constructed by professional graphic designers hired for the job, and we were quite pleased with its appearance and construction. Within a day of its erection in the museum, however, it was dismantled. The elaborate background structure was discarded and the photos and posters were placed on the wall in a display arrangement that made no presentation sense to the designers or to us. We were extremely disappointed and debated whether we should raise the matter with the local museum staff. By our standards, the reconstruction of the exhibit compromised its aesthetic integrity, to say nothing of the financial cost we had incurred personally. But we also learned a valuable lesson. If this was a partnership, and the museum staff had different notions regarding the presentation of the dialect exhibit, then why should they not have the prerogative to present the exhibit as they saw fit?

The incident also raised some deeper issues. What if they had changed the presentation in a way that led to linguistic error? What rights would we have had in the partnership? I'm not certain that I have an answer to these questions, but they clearly confront the issue of ownership in exercising the linguistic gratuity principle.

Issues of presentation about language diversity also arise in collaborative dialect awareness programs. By *presentation* I mean the selection of language issues to be highlighted and discussed within and outside the community. We have to admit that we decided these issues for Ocracoke and for the Lumbee community based on our expert status rather than by popular community determination. In the case of Ocracoke, we were concerned about the moribund status of the dialect and therefore stressed a theme of dialect endangerment. Our ethnographic interviews on island identity and the recession of the dialect, however, indicated that few islanders overtly associated the dialect directly with membership in the Ocracoke community, and that island residents did not necessarily share our concern for the recession of the dialect. The fact of the matter is that language issues are simply not paramount to islanders, who are much more concerned about economic and environmental issues such as property taxes, development, and ecology. Our portrayal of the recession of the traditional dialect sometimes evokes sympathetic and nostalgic responses by islanders when we talk about the changing status of the dialect, but our focus is also viewed as a bit of an oddity. As one islander who worked with us closely for almost a decade put it in an interview to a newspaper reporter, "The only person who worries about the dialect is Walt Wolfram."

In the case of Lumbee English, our focus has been on the symbolic ethnic and cultural identity of the variety. To some residents with a strong sense of Lumbee identity this focus has struck a respondent chord, since our research and programs acknowledge a unique, symbolic linguistic identity. Although I have received scores of supportive personal responses from members of the community thanking me for programs that help raise the consciousness of Lumbee identity, I have also received a few sharply negative reactions that seize on the portrayal of vernacular language as emblematic of identity when, in the opinion of the respondent, it simply projects a parody of "illiteracy and ignorance" unbefitting and unrepresentative of the many accomplishments of Lumbee people in mainstream culture. While we might dismiss such responses as uninformed manifestation of the principle of linguistic inferiority, they do reflect one interpretation of language diversity within the community. Furthermore, this entrenched attitude among some educational leaders within the community has caused us to go slowly in developing formal curricular materials for the schools on dialects and Lumbee English.

To some extent, the size of the community plays a role in the level of involvement and the rate of progression in the development of formal materials in these two communities. With approximately three hundred native residents and one K–12 school in Ocracoke, the role of personal relationships between researchers and community members has played to our advantage. Most residents know our work, and we have established genuine personal friendships with a number of residents over the years. By contrast, knowledge of our presence, purpose, and programs is much more limited in Robeson County. But community attitudes about language also differentiate the communities. Over the past several decades, Ocracoke has commodified its unique island status and has readily accepted and even embraced the notion of a distinct dialect heritage as a part of this commodification. Many residents have strongly supported the emphasis on preserving an eroding traditional lifestyle that includes their unique dialect. The community itself, including some of the educators and community leaders, seems primed to confront the linguistic inferiority principle, although the members may have been conflicted by the myth that they were speaking Shakespearean English, a prestigious dialect of English. By contrast, the linguistic inferiority principle, buoyed by an underlying racial ideology affecting Native Americans, seems much more entrenched in the Lumbee community.

One of the riskiest presentation ventures we have engaged in involves cooperation with the media. As Johnson (2001:592) notes, "scientists themselves have much to learn from the reception of their ideas by those outside their area of expertise," including their reception by the media. On several occasions, we talked to journalists and introduced them to community residents who have been quite friendly and helpful to them. Our rationale has been to portray dialect heritage in a positive public light for those who don't know about it or who don't recognize language as an important part of a traditional sociohistorical heritage. But such cooperation is admittedly a high-risk venture, and there are no guarantees of how the people and their language might be portrayed. For example, a couple of published stories on language in these communities have been based on erroneous assumptions and even stereotypes. On one occasion, a BBC correspondent in search of Elizabethan English on Ocracoke proposed getting some residents to read Shakespeare on camera. Although we strongly advised him not to ask islanders to do so, we later came upon one of our island friends, Rex O'Neal, standing on the dock in front of the television camera reading Shakespeare.[2] On the one hand, we had a good laugh, especially at the ironic parody of Rex gesticulating dramatically and reading Shakespeare with a contrived British accent; we jokingly referred to the performance as "Rex-speare." On the other hand, however, we had to admit that in our zeal to publicize language issues relating to the Ocracoke dialect, we probably played into the hands of those perpetuating stereotypes about the dialect as Elizabethan English.

One of our most gratifying experiences involving community empowerment on Ocracoke took place when the editorial staff of the school newspaper decided to feature the Brogue in one of their editions. We researchers were interviewed and the student staff presented dialect issues from their perspective. Also included were essays and poems about language written by students at the school from their own perspectives. This project was completely initiated by the students and teachers in the school rather than suggested by us.

Presentation issues are closely related to issues of representation—the ways in which a local dialect is characterized and commodified. How do we depict the dialect in our popular portrayals? For example, feature stories in journalistic accounts typically draw attention to sample dialect lexical items (e.g., words like *mommuck* 'harass', *meehonkey* 'hide and seek', and *dingbatter* 'non-islander' for Ocracoke and words like *juvember* 'slingshot', *ellick* 'coffee', and *brickhouse Indian* 'privileged Lumbee' for Lumbee English) even though our research focus is on phonological and morphosyntactic phenomena rather than the lexicon. Early in our research we compiled a dialect dictionary for local distribution in both communities under discussion here. The rationales for producing dictionaries early in the study of a dialect community are that (1) it is a tangible product that a local community can understand with minimal background information; (2) it can be produced as an ongoing project within a relatively short time frame, thus showing immediate results; and (3) it can involve local residents meaningfully in the collection of data and in some aspects of the compilation process. At the same time, linguists tend to scoff at popular, amateurish attempts by nonspecialists to capture local lexical items that mix pronunciation, eye dialect, and other associated sayings collected on an informal, impressionistic basis. Have we patronized or even misled the community by engaging in such activities, or have we simply found a common ground of interest in language variation? And have we compromised the activities of serious, painstaking lexical collections such as the *Dictionary of American Regional English* (Cassidy 1986, 1991, 1996) by engaging in rapid-fire production of dialect dictionaries? These are not insignificant questions in terms of balancing professional and community concerns as we represent the dialect to the community and to outsiders.

In most cases, social dialectologists also tend to portray more marked and vernacular versions of dialect—the more "exotic" and traditional forms of language variation—in their representations to wider audiences, including audiences of fellow linguists. At the same time that we preach about the variable nature of socially diagnostic linguistic features in our texts and in our classrooms, our dialect awareness materials run the danger of creating oversimplified caricatures that defy the authentic complexity of variation in the dialect community. The general public is not the only population that may have a tendency to create stereotypes. As Rickford (1997) points out, the themes that researchers highlight in their presentations may serve to reinforce or even create new kinds of stereotypes about the lives and language of a speech community. One of the stereotypes that social dialectologists have to guard against is the basilectal stereotype, where vernacular dialects are portrayed in their maximally vernacular form. Though often unconsciously, our portrayals are shaped by how we wish our information to be perceived and received.

In researcher-community collaboration, we can expect to encounter conflicting beliefs and values about language that may differentiate community members and the professional linguists who study them. As professional linguists, we are quite prepared to counter popular beliefs about the systematic patterning of vernacular dialects and the logic of these dialects in the name of the principle of error correction (Labov 1982). But how do we honestly but diplomatically confront a community leader responsible for our social networking in the community who offers the following assessment: "We had a linguist here a couple of years ago who tried to tell us our speech wasn't just Old English—we had to set him straight"? How do partnerships really work when community members and linguistic researchers enter into a partnership with different belief systems and entrenched ideologies about language diversity—the typical case when dealing with vernacular-speaking communities? How do we present findings that might describe racist and sexist attitudes as a part of the essential social background for understanding language variation when the researcher is committed to sharing information with community members? Is it ethical for a dialect awareness program to modify information for different audiences in order to "protect" our collaborative interests? These are difficult questions with no easy answers, but they affect the sharing of knowledge and researcher-community partnerships in significant ways. While we may assert that information is worth sharing with the community, the process of sharing is locally situated. Not all information is useful to a community, and the community may not be particularly interested in all the intricate details of information acquired by the researcher. Sharing information is a negotiated process and is typically programmed in a selective way to fit the needs and demands of the community as well as the collaborative partnership.

Finally, there is the issue of need and profit. Do communities really want and need our collaboration? Who really profits from our participation in the community? In our dialect awareness programs we have been careful not only to invest intellectually and socially in the Ocracoke and Lumbee communities but to invest financially as well. In both communities, we have ensured that the majority of financial revenues from our products go to local agencies such as the Ocracoke Preservation Society and the Museum of the Native American Resource Center. Though we have not profited economically, we can hardly claim that we have no profit motive. We have profited greatly from the communities we have researched—with respect to our professional advancement, our publication record, and the recognition we have received for proactive involvement with local communities (Rickford 1997:184). Even if we took a position that returning favors to communities should be limited to activities unrelated to language (e.g., babysitting, tutoring, or other volunteer activities in host communities), our motives for offering such services might be suspect.

We honestly feel that awareness about dialect diversity and the symbolic role of language variation in reflecting cultural heritage has been heightened through our involvement in the community. Was this a mutual goal derived from the partnership or simply an imposition of our sociolinguistic and sociopolitical agenda and belief system on the community? It is apparent that there are many issues that need to be contemplated in advocating researcher-community partnerships, the application of the linguistic gratuity principle, and the implementation of dialect awareness programs. The discussion here is neither comprehensive nor complete; in many respects we are just starting to consider the implications of sharing knowledge and expertise with host research communities in the name of linguistic gratuity. Perhaps the most instructive aspect of this reflection is the self-revelation of the inequality of the partnership and the professional capital present in these types of advocacy relationships. Furthermore, relationships of empowerment remain an elusive ideal given the differential status of language researchers and community members, as well as the prevailing language ideologies in society with respect to vernacular language varieties. Nonetheless, it seems that returning linguistic favors in some form is a good and proper thing to consider when we have mined the speech community's linguistic resources to our advantage.

I must confess that one of the things that has appealed to me about sociolinguistics over the years is the opportunities it offers for carrying out research that may address social issues and problems. The construction of dialect awareness programs for and with the local community has represented one such opportunity. Even if these programs may not be as altruistically motivated as I once thought, they still seem to be a worthy endeavor that can profit both the community and the social science researcher in a synergistic way. At the same time, we need to be aware of and honestly confront the issues that arise in the implementation of these programs.

## NOTES

Support for the projects reported here came from NSF Grant No BCS-9910224, a grant to the Ocracoke Preservation Society by the Outer Banks Foundation, and the William C. Friday Endowment. Special thanks are due to Natalie Schilling-Estes, Kirk Hazen, and Clare Dannenberg, who offered insight based on their experience with these respective projects. Most of all, I am greatly indebted to my friends and acquaintances in Ocracoke and in Robeson County. I feel most fortunate to have worked in communities that are more tolerant and forgiving than we could rightly expect given our sometimes invasive attempts to work collaboratively in the implementation of dialect awareness programs.

1. Parts of this section are adapted from Wolfram 1998.

2. We have departed from usual procedure of protecting the anonymity of subjects here, since Rex O'Neal wishes to be known by his real name in published references. For a discussion of the performance style of Rex O'Neal see Schilling-Estes 1998.

## REFERENCES

Baratz, Joan C. 1968. Language in the Economically Disadvantaged Child. *ASHA* 10 (April): 143–45.

Baugh, John. 2001. *Beyond Ebonics: Linguistic Pride and Racial Prejudice*. New York: Oxford University Press.

Blanton, Phyllis, and Karen Waters, producers. 1995. *The Ocracoke Brogue*. Raleigh: North Carolina Language and Life Project.

Blommaert, Jan, ed. 1999. *Language Ideological Debates*. Berlin: Mouton de Gruyter.

Briggs, Charles L. 1986. *Learning to Ask: A Sociolinguistic Appraisal of the Role of the Interview in Social Science Research*. New York: Cambridge University Press.

Cameron, Deborah, Elizabeth Frazer, Penelope Harvey, M. B. H. Rampton, and Kay Richardson. 1992. *Researching Language: Issues of Power and Method*. London: Routledge.

Cassidy, Frederic, general ed. 1986, 1991, 1996. *Dictionary of American Regional English*, Vols. 1–3. Cambridge: Harvard University Press/Belknap.

Dannenberg, Clare. 2002. *Sociolinguistic Constructs of Ethnic Identity: The Syntactic Delineation of a Native American Variety*. Publication of the American Dialect Society, no. 87. Durham: Duke University Press.

Donmall, B. G., ed. 1985. *Language Awareness: National Council for Language in Education Reports and Papers*. London: CILT.

Farr-Whiteman, Marcia, ed. 1980. *Reactions to Ann Arbor: Vernacular Black English and Education*. Washington, D.C.: Center for Applied Linguistics.

Hammonds, Renee. 2000. *People's Perceptions of Lumbee Vernacular English.* M.A. thesis, North Carolina Central University, Durham.

Heller, Monica, John Rickford, Marty Laforest, and Danielle Cyr. 1999. Sociolinguistics and Public Debate. *Journal of Sociolinguistics* 3:260–88.

Hutcheson, Neal, and Walt Wolfram, producers. 2000. *Indian by Birth: The Lumbee Dialect.* Raleigh: North Carolina Language and Life Project.

Johnson, Sally. 2001. Who's Misunderstanding Whom? Sociolinguistics, Public Debate, and the Media. *Journal of Sociolinguistics* 5:591–610.

Kerns, Ursulla H. 2001. *A Comparison of Lexical Items in Lumbee Vernacular English from the Pembroke and Prospect Communities.* M.A. thesis, North Carolina Central University, Durham.

Labov, William. 1970. The Logic of Nonstandard English. In *Georgetown Monograph Series on Languages and Linguistics* No. 22, ed. James E. Alatis, pp. 1–41. Washington, D.C.: Georgetown University.

———. 1982. Objectivity and Commitment in Linguistic Science: The Case of the Black English Trial in Ann Arbor. *Language in Society* 11:165–201.

Locklear, Hayes Alan, Walt Wolfram, Natalie Schilling-Estes, and Clare Dannenberg. 1999. *A Dialect Dictionary of Lumbee English.* Raleigh: North Carolina Language and Life Project.

Milroy, James. 2001. Language Ideologies and the Consequences of Standardization. *Journal of Sociolinguistics* 5:530–55.

*Ocracoke Speaks: The Distinct Sounds of the "Hoi Toide" Brogue.* 1999. Raleigh: Ocracoke Preservation Society and North Carolina Language and Life Project.

Rickford, John R. 1997. Unequal Partnerships: Sociolinguistics and the African American Speech Community. *Language in Society* 26:161–97.

———. 1999. *African American Vernacular English: Features, Evolution, and Educational Implications.* Malden, Mass.: Blackwell.

Schilling-Estes, Natalie. 1998. Investigating Self-Conscious Speech: The Performance Register in Ocracoke English. *Language in Society* 28:53–83.

Wolfram, Walt. 1969. *A Linguistic Description of Detroit Negro Speech.* Washington, D.C.: Center for Applied Linguistics.

———. 1970. Linguistic Premises and the Nature of Nonstandard Dialects. *Speech Teacher* (September): 176–86.

———. 1974. *Sociolinguistic Aspects of Assimilation: Puerto Rican English in New York City.* Washington, D.C.: Center for Applied Linguistics.

———. 1993. Ethical Considerations in Language Awareness Programs. *Issues in Applied Linguistics* 4:225–55.

———. 1998. Scrutinizing Linguistic Gratuity. Journal of Sociolinguistics: A View from the Field. *Journal of Sociolinguistics* 2:271–79.

Wolfram, Walt, Carolyn Temple Adger, and Donna Christian. 1999. *Dialects in Schools and Communities.* Mahweh, N.J.: Erlbaum.

Wolfram, Walt, and Donna Christian. 1976. *Appalachian Speech.* Arlington, Va.: Center for Applied Linguistics.

Wolfram, Walt Clare Dannenberg, Stanley Knick, and Linda Oxendine. 2002. *Fine in the World: Lumbee Language in Time and Place*. Raleigh: North Carolina State Humanities Extension/Publications.

Wolfram, Walt, and Natalie Schilling-Estes. 1995. Moribund Dialects and the Endangerment Canon: The Case of the Ocracoke Brogue. *Language* 71:696–721.

———. 1997. *Hoi Toide on the Outer Banks: The Story of the Ocracoke Brogue*. Chapel Hill: University of North Carolina Press.

———. 1998. *American English: Dialects and Variation*. Malden/Oxford: Blackwell.

Wolfram, Walt, Natalie Schilling-Estes, and Kirk Hazen. 1995. *Dialects and the Ocracoke Brogue*. 8th grade curriculum, Ocracoke School. Raleigh: North Carolina Language and Life Project.

Wolfram, Walt, and Erik R. Thomas. 2002. *The Development of African American English*. Malden, Mass.: Blackwell.

Wolfram, Walt, Kirk Hazen, and Natalie Schilling-Estes. 1999. *Dialect Change and Maintenance on the Outer Banks*. Publication of the American Dialect Society, no. 81. Tuscaloosa: University of Alabama Press.

# Multilingualism in the South: A Carolinas Case Study

*Blair A. Rudes*

A widely held misconception about the American South is that it is, and has always been, an essentially monolingual, English-speaking region. The truth, however, is that in the early colonial period, from the early sixteenth century to the mid–eighteenth century, the South was one of the most linguistically diverse areas in North America—a place where more different languages were spoken than anywhere else except California. Although English did become the lingua franca and the dominant language from the mid–eighteenth century onward, other languages were always spoken in the region. With the economic prosperity that has characterized the New South in the later part of the twentieth century and the opening of the twenty-first century, the region has become a mecca for immigrants seeking to better their lives. As a result, the linguistic diversity of the South is growing at the fastest rate in the nation. I will illustrate the changing linguistic face of the South by examining the history of multilingualism in North and South Carolina.

## AT THE DAWN OF RECORDED HISTORY

The documented history of the Carolinas began in the early sixteenth century with a text entitled "Testimony of Francisco de Chicora" (Swanton 1922: 32–46; 1940). "Testimony" contained recollections of dinner conversations regarding Spanish explorations of the southern coast of North America prior to 1521. The dinner conversations occurred in Santo Domingo, Cuba, and among the participants was an Indian—Francisco de Chicora—who had been captured in a slave raid at Winyah Bay and made the household servant of Lucas Vázquez de Ayllón, the man who had financed the slave raid (Caruso 1963:20). The "testimony" of Francisco de Chicora is difficult to interpret; however, the Indian names given for places and things in the account clearly show that the Spanish had explored the Carolinas at least as far north as Pamlico Sound by the 1520s and that several different languages were spoken in the region (Rudes 2002). For example, the testimony gives the word *xathi* for 'another cereal [other than maize]' that grew in the land called Duharhe, an area explored by the Spanish. Swanton (1940) believed that the word referred to beans, which were commonly grown along with corn. The only language in the Southeast that has a word for 'beans' that resembles Spanish *xathi* is Tuscarora, a Northern Iroquoian language spoken just to the west of Pamlico Sound, in which the word is *θáheʔ* (Rudes 1999: 409). Also, the name for one of the "gods" of the people of Duharhe is given in the testimony as Quexuga, 'great sovereign of the southern region,' which appears to be the same word as found in the Algonquian language spoken on the barrier islands of Pamlico Sound, Roanoke *kewás* 'god,' *kewasówak* 'gods' (Hariot 1590: folio E3).

More comprehensive documentation from explorations in the sixteenth century by Hernando de Soto, Juan Pardo, Francisco Fernandez de Ecija, and René Laudonnière, the seventeenth century by Maurice Mathews and John Lederer, and the early eighteenth century by John Lawson revealed that the Carolinas were home to peoples who spoke more than ten different languages from four different language families (Ecija 1605; Lederer 1672; Lawson 1709; Cheves 1897:186–87, 201, 249; Waddell 1980; Hudson 1990; Clayton, Knight, and Moore 1993; Martin [forthcoming]; Rudes, Blumer, and May [forthcoming]). The area around Albemarle and Pamlico Sound was home to peoples who spoke languages belonging to the Algonquian family (Chowan, Machapunga, and Pamlico). Inland along the coastal plain between the Neuse and the Roanoke Rivers, as well as in the western mountains, were spoken languages belonging to the Iroquoian family (Tuscarora, Meherrin, and Cherokee). The southern coast between the Santee and Savannah Rivers was home to peoples who spoke languages belonging to the Cusaboan family (Ashepoo, Cussao, Edisto, Escamacu, and Etiwan). Elsewhere in the Carolinas—on the piedmont, in the Sandhills, and on the coast and coastal plain between the Santee and the Neuse Rivers—were spoken languages belonging to the Catawban family (Catawba, Esaw, Santee, Saraw, Sewee, Sugaree, Wateree, and Woccon).

In the seventeenth and early eighteenth centuries, the Carolinas became home to peoples who spoke Indian languages from two other families not native to the area: the Muskogean family, represented by Yamassee in South Carolina, which had been spoken earlier to the southwest along the Altamaha River in Georgia; and the Siouan family, represented by Occaneechi, Saponi, Shakori, and Tutelo in North Carolina, which had been spoken earlier in southern Virginia. In addition, Natchez and Yuchi, two language isolates (i.e., languages not belonging to any known language family) from other parts of the South, came to be spoken in the Carolinas (Martin [forthcoming]; Rudes, Blumer, and May [forthcoming]; Waddell [forthcoming]).

## THE IMPACT OF COLONIZATION

It was not long after Soto's expedition through the Carolinas in 1540 that the French set out to establish a beachfront in the South. In 1562, the French explored from the mouth of the Santee River south to the Savannah River and established a fort—Charlesfort—in Port Royal Sound near present-day Charleston, South Carolina. However, during the winter of 1563 the soldiers stationed at the fort, having run short of food, mutinied and abandoned the fort. Thus ended the brief foray into the Carolinas by the French (Laudonnière 1562; Waddell 1980).

The Spanish did not just explore the Carolinas; they established what they hoped would be permanent forts and missions in the area. The first fort was established in 1565 at Santa Helena, near present-day Beaufort, South Carolina (Hudson 1990:3). Pardo later established forts in five Catawban villages in the interior of the Carolinas (Hudson 1990:146). The first Spanish mission to the Carolina Indians was established around 1567 by Pardo's chaplain, Father Sebastian Montero, at Wateree on the North Carolina piedmont (Hudson 1990:153). As a result of these sixteenth-century ventures, the chorus of native voices in the Carolinas was joined by Spanish, but not for long. Dissatisfied with their treatment at the hands of the Spanish, the Indians became hostile, eventually driving the Spanish to abandon their interior forts by 1568. Although the Spanish maintained the fort at Santa Helena for a while, Indian hostility and increasing pressures from English colonies to the north forced the Spanish to retreat southward out of the Carolinas by the end of the seventeenth century (Hudson 1990: 177–81).

The French and Spanish attempts at colonizing the Carolinas were quickly followed by efforts by the English, whose first try was the ill-fated venture of Sir Walter Raleigh on Roanoke Island in 1585. Following the loss of that colony, the English did not venture into the Carolinas for another sixty years. In 1646, the Virginia colonists organized against the Indians along the Chowan River as the first step in a sustained effort to colonize the Chowan River region north of Albemarle Sound (Juricek 1964:153). In 1662, Captain John Hilton explored the area around Cape Fear, and in 1664 a group of New Englanders established a colony there by the name of Charles Town (South 1972:35). After a few years, the Cape Fear colonists began to have problems with the local Indians and abandoned the colony. Three years later in 1670, another English colony—also named Charles Town (present-day Charleston, South Carolina)—was established at the former site of the French settlement of Port Royal (Cheves 1897:186–87, 201, 249). It would be the first enduring English settlement in the Carolinas. Later in the century, colonists moved south out of Jamestown to establish communities around Albemarle Sound.

## THE LEGACY OF SERVITUDE AND SLAVERY

When the English established their first colonies in the Carolinas, they brought with them involuntary servants (prisoners) and indentured servants (landless and out-of-work peasants) to work their land and tend their households. These servants came from across the British Isles and included individuals whose native languages were Erse (Irish Gaelic), Cornish, Gaelic (Scots Gaelic), Manx, Scots, and Welsh, although nearly all spoke English as well. There is no evidence that these non-English languages left an enduring imprint on the speech of the Carolinas.

During the late seventeenth century, the servant workforce was augmented by captured Indians and Africans. However, not until the 1697 breakup of the Royal African Company monopoly on the slave trade did large numbers of Africans enter the Carolinas in servitude (Feldmeth 1988). The slaves brought with them their native West African languages (e.g., Bambara, Igbo, Malinké, Songhay, Twi, Wolof, Yoruba), as well as African-African, African-Spanish, and African-English pidgins (trader vocabularies) that evolved out of necessity for communication among the Africans who spoke different languages and their Spanish and English captors. The presence of African languages on Carolina soil is attested by the local preservation, to the present day, of certain vocabulary items such as *cooter* 'terrapin' from Bambara and Malinké *kuta* 'turtle' in the Sandhills area (Locklear, Wolfram, Schilling-Estes, and Dannenberg 1999:2).

What happened next is a subject of debate among linguists. Under one scenario, labeled the "Creolist" view, the pidgins the Africans brought to the Carolinas evolved over time into an English-based creole language, a remnant of which is the Gullah language spoken to this day on the Atlantic islands off the coast of South Carolina. As the speakers of the creole continued to have extensive contact with English speakers, but little or no contact with speakers of African languages, the creole evolved further in the direction of the regional standard English. In another scenario, called the "Anglicist" view, the African slaves, working side by side with the prisoners and indentured servants who had preceded them, abandoned their African languages and African-based pidgins in favor of the lower-class, prison-jargon-laced English of their co-workers. Regardless of what actually transpired, the end result was the same: the speech of African slaves became intelligible to the white population in the area, but distinctively different from that population's speech.

## THE SPREAD OF ENGLISH IN THE EIGHTEENTH CENTURY

As European and African languages were introduced into the South, the native Indian languages did not all at once disappear. Rather, the demise of native linguistic diversity occurred by inches as communities were decimated by foreign diseases, European-introduced alcohol, intertribal conflicts, and forced relocations to make room for ever-expanding European settlement. The growth of the English colonies along the Carolina coast had already taken a toll on the indigenous communities, in particular the coastal Algonquians, by the opening of the eighteenth century. Native losses in the Tuscarora Wars of 1711–13 and the Yamassee War of 1715 further reduced the coastal Indian populations, as well as the populations of tribes farther inland. A major result of these conflicts was the opening of the interior of the Carolinas to English settlement (Rudes et al. [forthcoming]).

The remaining Indian population took refuge in four major areas: the Blue Ridge Mountains, the Catawba-Wateree River valley, the upper Pee Dee River tributaries, and the reservation in Bertie County, North Carolina, set aside for the Tuscaroras who remained in North Carolina after the Tuscarora Wars. Located in the far west of the Carolinas in the rugged

Blue Ridge Mountains, the Cherokees remained relatively untouched by English expansion until late in the eighteenth century, and their language continued to flourish. Numerous other Indian communities whose homes had been on the piedmont and coastal plain also moved west to escape English settlement, reestablishing their villages in the Catawba-Wateree River valley. By the mid–eighteenth century, the valley was home to more than twenty Indian communities who "each had their own dialect [language]" and who had come there from all over the Carolinas and elsewhere, including the Catawba, Eno, Esaw, Keyauwee, Kussoe, Natchez, Saponi, Saraw, Sugaree, Suteree, Wateree, and Yamassee (Adair 1775:225; Rudes et al. [forthcoming]). Over time, the language differences within the Catawba-Wateree Valley were leveled in favor of two Catawba dialects—Esaw and Saraw—which continued to be spoken into the twentieth century (Rudes 2003).

Meanwhile, Indians from such communities as Cape Fear, Cheraw, Pedee, Saxapahaw, Shakori, Tuscarora, Waccamaw, and Winyaw "hid out" along the upper Pee Dee, Lumber, Lynches, and Waccamaw Rivers. Apparently, the use of the native languages by these people died out completely in favor of English sometime in the eighteenth century, for there is no record of native languages being spoken along these rivers after the late eighteenth century (Rudes et al. [forthcoming]). In Bertie County, the Tuscarora were joined by remnants of other tribes from the North Carolina and Virginia coastal plain, including the Meherrin (Rudes 1981).

In addition to the relatively large Indian communities in the four areas mentioned above, isolated Indian communities and individual families remained scattered throughout the Carolinas in the eighteenth century. Some of these communities were located near English settlements (e.g., Sewee near Charleston), while others distanced themselves in remote locales. How long the native languages continued to be used is uncertain due to the lack of records; however, in all cases, the communities had shifted to the use of English by the late nineteenth and early twentieth centuries.

## TWO HUNDRED YEARS OF ENGLISH DOMINION

Between the mid–eighteenth century and the mid–twentieth century, English went unchallenged as the language of the Carolinas. The English-based creole of African American slaves shifted closer and closer to the regional standard English, eventually becoming so like English that it was considered simply a (substandard) dialect of the language.

Although various Indian languages continued to be spoken in isolated communities, a series of smallpox epidemics in the late eighteenth century and relocations (both voluntary and involuntary) to areas outside the Carolinas greatly reduced the number of speakers of these languages. Unquestionably, the greatest reduction occurred in 1838 with the forced removal of most Cherokees to Oklahoma, an event known as "The Trail of Tears" (Perdue and Green 1995). An even earlier removal occurred in 1803, when the Tuscaroras who had remained on the reservation in Bertie County finally gave in to the incessant white encroachment on their land, leased the remaining holdings, and moved to join their brethren on the Tuscarora reservation in New York State (Johnson 1968:2.195). By the mid–nineteenth century, only two areas remained where the concentration of Indians was large enough for the native languages to be preserved: the lower Catawba River valley around Rock Hill, South Carolina, where the Catawba language continued to be spoken into the first half of the twentieth century (Rudes 2003), and the mountains of western North Carolina, where Cherokee continues to be spoken to the present day.

Besides Catawba and Cherokee, the only language other than English to endure for any length of time in the Carolinas was German. Spoken in various communities established by immigrants from Pennsylvania and abroad, German was favored by the widespread use of the language in the original thirteen colonies (Crawford 1999). Nevertheless, even German gave way to English in the Carolinas by the latter half of the nineteenth century.

By the start of the twentieth century, the Carolinas were almost exclusively English speaking. Because such forces as industrialization and urbanization, which brought new immigrants to other parts of the United States in the late nineteenth and early twentieth centuries, had little impact on the Carolinas, the linguistic situation did not change until the middle of the twentieth century.

While the number of languages other than English spoken in the Carolinas between 1750 and 1950 declined dramatically, there was a countervailing increase in the diversity of English varieties spoken in the region. The early settlers brought with them the full range of English regional and social dialects spoken in the British Isles. Although these dialect differences surely underwent substantial leveling in the small early colonies, the western movement of settlers in the eighteenth century resulted in an expanded distribution of English speakers across a large and geographically diverse region that included barrier islands, the Atlantic coast, the coastal plain, the piedmont, the foothills, and the mountains, as well as numerous river systems. The geographic dispersion and resultant isolation of communities provided fertile ground for the evolution of regional dialects as local innovations occurred. Furthermore, the relatively rigid class distinctions of the antebellum South favored the preservation of social dialects brought over from England, as well as the development of new ones. In addition, as noted earlier, the earlier creolized English of African American slaves and Indians living in remote communities developed into unique variants. Thus, in a manner of speaking, the linguistic history of the Carolinas from 1750 to 1950 was one in which the diversity of languages was "exchanged" for a diversity of English vernaculars.

## A REEMERGENCE OF MULTILINGUALISM

In the 1940s and 1950s, the flow of migrant farm workers increased dramatically throughout the United States. While Mexican laborers were a major component of this workforce in the central and western parts of the country, they did not constitute a significant proportion of the migrant laborers in the East until the late 1960s. Between that time and the early 1990s, the number of Spanish-speaking migrant workers in the East increased exponentially, and, as elsewhere in the United States, some chose to "settle out of" the migrant stream and take up permanent residence. As a result, by the 1990s, settled-out migrant workers formed a major component of the non-English-speaking population in many parts of the Carolinas (Cox et al. 1992; Columbia Electronic Encyclopedia 2000).

Following the Vietnam War, immigration into the United States increased at such a pace that it threatened to overwhelm the resources of such traditional gateway communities as Boston, Miami, New York, San Francisco, and Seattle. As a result, the federal government implemented a policy of encouraging immigrants to settle in communities elsewhere in the United States. This change in policy brought significant numbers of non-English speakers from Southeast Asia and other parts of the world to the Carolinas, in particular to the larger urban areas.

The flow of non-English speakers took another dramatic upswing in the late 1980s and 1990s as a result of the radical changes in economic development and social policies in the region—changes that created the

"New South." Immigrants poured into the region to reap the benefits of economic prosperity. Evidence of the phenomenal impact of immigration on the linguistic picture of the Carolinas comes from enrollment figures for limited-English-proficient (LEP) students in the public schools. North Carolina had 4,586 LEP students in grades K–12 of the public schools in the 1989–90 school year out of a total enrollment of 1,131,244 students. By the 1999–2000 school year, the number of LEP students had risen to 41,667—a 908.6% increase—while the overall enrollment had risen only to 1,275,925 students—a 12.8% increase. In South Carolina, the LEP student population in the public schools grew from 1,466 during the 1991–92 school year to 5,577 in 1999–2000, a 280.4% increase, while the total enrollment actually decreased by 5.1% from 684,753 to 650,450 students. The growth in the LEP student enrollments in both North and South Carolina far exceeded the overall 105% increase nationwide during the same time period (from 2,154,781 LEP students in the 1989–1990 school year to 4,416,580 in 1999–2000) (NCELA 2002).

The limited-English-proficient individuals in the Carolinas in the year 2000 came from a variety of linguistic backgrounds. As elsewhere in the United States, the vast majority—72% in North Carolina and 73% in South Carolina—spoke Spanish as their first language. Languages spoken by the remaining portion of the LEP population included Arabic, Chinese, Greek, Hindi, Hmong, Japanese, Khmer (Cambodian), Korean, Lao, Portuguese, Russian, Serbo-Croatian, Tagalog, Vietnamese, and a host of other languages (NCELA 2002). At the same time, the Eastern Band of Cherokee Indians and the Catawba Indian Nation were engaged in major efforts to preserve, restore, and revitalize the Cherokee and Catawba languages in the Carolinas. Thus, by the opening of the twenty-first century, the Carolinas could once again rightly be called a multilingual region.

## SUMMARY

The Carolinas have always been a linguistically diverse region; the fertile land and mild climate of the area have attracted immigrants speaking different languages since time immemorial. When Europeans first set foot on Carolina soil in the early sixteenth century, the land was home to Indians who spoke around a dozen mutually unintelligible languages. European colonists brought Spanish, French, German, and English to the mix, and African slaves added a variety of West African languages and African-based pidgins. Shortly before the War of Independence, colonial successes in conflicts with the native population resulted in an expansion of English-speaking settlements into the interior and made English the lingua franca and, ultimately, the dominant language of the region. Concurrent with the rise of English to supremacy, the number of speakers of non-English languages, including the native Indian languages, declined rapidly.

For the next two hundred years, from the middle of the eighteenth century until the middle of the twentieth century, the Carolinas appeared to outsiders to be an entirely monolingual English-speaking area; however, a closer look reveals that non-English languages continued to be spoken in isolated pockets, with aboriginal Indian languages surviving into the twenty-first century. Furthermore, even the English spoken in the area was rich in linguistic diversity, exhibiting a wide range of regional, social, ethnic, and racial dialects.

In the second half of the twentieth century, economic and social changes greatly affected the linguistic composition of the area. The influx of migrant farm workers, post–Vietnam War refugee resettlement, and immigration that resulted from economic development in the New South has thousands of non-English speakers making the Carolinas their new home each year. As the twenty-first century opens, the Carolinas are well on their way to reclaiming their status as among the most linguistically diverse regions in North America.

## REFERENCES

Adair, James. 1775. *The History of the American Indians*. London: E. and C. Dilly.

Calloway, Colin G. 1999. *First Peoples: A Documentary Survey of American Indian History*. Boston: Bedford Books of St. Martin's Press.

Caruso, John Anthony. 1963. *The Southern Frontier.* Indianapolis: Bobbs-Merrill.

Cheves, Langdon, ed. 1897. The Shaftesbury Papers and Other Records Relating to the Carolinas and the First Settlement on the Ashley River Prior to the Year 1676. *Collections of the South Carolina Historical Society* 5:1–523.

Clayton, Lawrence R., Vernon James Knight Jr., and Edward C. Moore, eds. 1993. *The De Soto Chronicles: The Expedition of Hernando de Soto to North America in 1539–1543.* 2 vols. Tuscaloosa: University of Alabama Press.

Columbia Electronic Encyclopedia. 2000. Migrant Labor. http://www.factmonster .com/ce6/bus/A0833129.html, accessed 11 July 2002.

Cox, John L., Graham Burkheimer, Thomas R. Curtin, Blair A. Rudes, Robert Iachan, William Strang, Elisabeth Carlson, George Zarkin, and Nora Dean. 1992. *Descriptive Study of the Chapter 1 Migrant Education Program: Final Report.* Research Triangle Park, N.C.: Research Triangle Institute.

Crawford, James. 1999. Bilingual Education: History, Politics, Theory, and Practice. http://ourworld.compuserve.com/homepages/JWCRAWFORD/BECh1.htm, accessed 11 July 2002.

Ecija, Francisco Fernandez de. 1605. Testimonio del viaje que hizo el Capitan Francisco Fernandez de Ecija a la visita de la costa de la Canada del Norte de este pressidio / año 1605. In Lowery (n.d.).

Feldmeth, Greg D. 1988. Slavery in the American Colonies. http://home.earthlink.net/~gfeldmeth/slave.html, accessed 11 July 2002.

Haklvyt, R. 1600. *The Voyages, Navigations, Traffiques, and Discoueries of the English Nation, and in some few places, where they haue not been, of strangers, performed within and before the time of these hundred yeeres, to all parts of the Newfound world of America, or the West Indies. from 73. degrees of Northerly to 57. of Southerly latitude: As namely to Engronland, Meta Incognita, Estotiland, Tierra de Labrador, Newfoundland, vp The grand bay, the gulfe of S. Laurence, and the Riuer of Canada to Hochelaga and Saguenay, along the coast of Arambec, to the shores and maines of Virginia and Florida, and on the West or backside of them both, to the rich and pleasant countries or Nueua Biscaya, Cibola, Teguex, Cicuic, Quiuira, to the 15. prouinces of the kingdome of New Mexico, to the botttome of the gulfe of California, and vp the Riuer of Buena Guia: And likewise to all the yles both small and great lying before the cape of Florida, The bay of Mexico and Tierra firma, to the coasts and Inlands of Newe Spaine, Tierra firma, and Guiana, vp the mighty Riuers of Orenoque, Dessekobe, and Marannon, to euery part of the coast of Brasil, to the Riuer of Plate, through the Streights of Magellan forward and backward, and to the South of the said Steights as farre as 57. degrees: And from thence on the backside of America, along the coastes, harbours, and capes of Chili, Peru, Nicaragua, Nueua Espanna, Nueua Galicia, Culiacan, California, Noua Albion, and more Northerly as farre as 43 degrees: Together with the two reknowned, and prosperous voyages of Sir Francis Drake and M. Thomas Candish round about the circuference of the whole earth, and diuers other voyages intended and set forth for that course.* London: George Bishop, Ralfe Newberie, and Robert Baker.

Hariot, Thomas. 1590. *The Briefe and True Report of the New Found Land of Virginia.* London: Theodore de Bry.

Hudson, Charles M. 1990. *The Juan Pardo Expeditions: Explorations of the Carolinas and Tennessee, 1566–1568, with Documents Relating to the Pardo Expeditions Transcribed, Translated, and Annotated by Paul E. Hoffman.* Washington, D.C.: Smithsonian Institution.

Johnson, F. Roy. 1968. *The Tuscaroras.* 2 vols. Murfreesboro, N.C.: Johnson.

Juricek, J. T. 1964. The Westo Indians. *Ethnohistory* 11(2):134–73.

Kindler, Anneka L. 2002. *Survey of the States' Limited English Proficient Students and Available Educational Programs and Services, 1999–2000: Summary Report*. Washington, D.C.: National Clearinghouse for English Language Acquisition and Language Instruction Educational Programs.

Laudonnière, René. 1562. "The description of the *VVest Indies* in generall, but chiefly and particularly of *Florida*" and Ribaut's First Voyage to Florida. In Haklvyt 1600, vol. 3, pp. 304–19.

Lawson, John. 1709. *A New Voyage to Carolina, Containing the Exact Description and Natural History of that Country, Together with the Present State Thereof, and a Journal of a Thousand Miles, Travelled Through Several Nations of Indians, Giving a Particular Account of Their Customs, Manners, Etc*. London.

Lederer, John. 1672. *The Discoveries of John Lederer, Collected and Translated from his Discoveries and Writings by Sir William Talbot, Lord*. London: Printed for Samuel Heyrick.

Locklear, Hayes Alan, Walt Wolfram, Natalie Schilling-Estes, and Clare Dannenberg. 1999. *A Dialect Dictionary of Lumbee English*. Raleigh: North Carolina Language and Life Project.

Lowery, Woodbury. N.d. The Spanish Settlements within the Present Limits of the United States, vol. 5. MS. Library of Congress Manuscript Division, Washington, D.C.

Martin, Jack. Forthcoming. Southeastern Languages. In *Handbook of North American Indians*. Volume 14: *Southeast*, ed. Raymond Fogelson. Washington, D.C.: Smithsonian Institution.

NCELA. 2002. State Data. Washington, D.C.: National Clearinghouse on English Language Acquisition and Language Instruction Educational Programs. http://ncbe/gwu.edu, accessed 11 July 2002.

Perdue, Theda, and Michael D. Green, eds. 1995. *The Cherokee Removal: A Brief History with Documents*. Boston: Bedford Books of St. Martin's Press.

Rudes, Blair A. 1981. Cowinchahakon/Akawę̨čʔá:ka:ʔ: The Meherrin in the Nineteenth Century. *Algonquian and Iroquoian Linguistics* 6(3):5–7.

Rudes, Blair A. 2002. The First Description of an Iroquoian People: The Spanish among the Tuscarora before 1521. Paper presented at the Conference on Iroquois Research. Rensselaerville, New York.

Rudes, Blair A. 2003. Catawba Phonemes. In *Essays in Algonquian, Catawban, and Siouan Linguistics in Memory of Frank T. Siebert, Jr.*, ed. Blair A. Rudes and David J. Costa, pp. 217–53. Algonquian and Iroquoian Linguistics, Memoir 16. Winnipeg: University of Manitoba Linguistics Department.

Rudes, Blair A., Thomas J. Blumer, and J. Alan May. Forthcoming. Catawba. In *Handbook of North American Indians*. Volume 14: *Southeast*, ed. Raymond Fogelson. Washington, D.C.: Smithsonian Institution.

South, Stanley. 1972. *Tribes of the Carolina Lowland: Pedee-Sewee-Winyaw-Waccamaw-Cape Fear-Congaree-Wateree-Santee*. Columbia: University of South Carolina, Institute for Archaeology and Anthropology.

Swanton, John R. 1922. *Early History of the Creek Indians and Their Neighbors*. Bureau of American Ethnology Bulletin 73. Washington, D.C.: Government Printing Office.

Swanton, John R. 1940. The First Description of an Indian Tribe in the Territory of the Present United States. In *Studies for William A. Reed,* ed. Nathaniel M. Caffee and Thomas A. Kirby, pp. 326–28. New Orleans: Louisiana State University Press.

Taukchiray, Wes. 1983. North Carolina in the Fall of 1754 with the Emphasis on the American Indian Population. MS. South Carolina Historical Society, Charleston.

Waddell, Gene. 1980. *Indians of the South Carolina Lowcountry, 1562–1751*. Published for the Southern Studies Program, University of South Carolina. Spartanburg: Reprint Co.

Waddell, Gene. Forthcoming. Cusabo. In *Handbook of North American Indians*. Volume 14: *Southeast,* ed. Raymond Fogelson.Washington, D.C.: Smithsonian Institution.

# Defining Appalachian English

*Kirk Hazen and Ellen Fluharty*

In short, a Hill-Billie is a free and untrammeled white citizen of Alabama, who lives in the hills, has no means to speak of, dresses as he can, talks as he pleases, drinks whiskey when he gets it, and fires off his revolver as the fancy takes him. —*New York Evening Journal,* 1900, as cited in DARE 1991

I think them people up in Boston and New York and some of them places, I think they talk real funny. —Julie, 58, European American, Female

Language variation is by nature under social influence, but with some dialects the social pressures take on a life of their own. The myths and misperceptions about what Appalachian English is and what it means have persisted for over a century. The current result is that the popular image of Appalachian English is far removed from the language variation patterns that comprise the speech of native Appalachians (Hazen and Fluharty 2001). We present this study of Appalachian English to detail how its most popular incarnations have affected the people of Appalachia.

As a preliminary step, we bifurcate the term *Appalachian English* into two separate terms: *Appalachian Englishes,* referring to varieties of English spoken in Appalachia, and *Appalachian Drawl,* the popular language stereotype. In the first section of this chapter, we illustrate the key features of the Appalachian Drawl with materials taken from television, Internet, and newspapers. In the second section, we discuss the continuing conflict over whether Appalachia is socioculturally delimited or strictly a geographic region. In the third section, we qualitatively discuss the most prevalent vernacular features of Appalachian Englishes. We end by highlighting our speakers' attitudes about Appalachian Englishes and the pervasiveness of dialect discrimination.

From the outset, it should be noted that most people who are native to the Appalachian region are not influenced by the concept of *Appalachian*—they identify neither positively nor negatively with the Appalachian region as an entity—although more local, regional identification is normal. It is true that natives know of the term and the stereotypes, but there is little indication that these are ideas with which people consciously identify. An example of this is Julie, quoted in the second epigraph, who was raised in Steubenville, Ohio. She does not consider herself Appalachian even though her parents are from Appalachian Kentucky and she has spent her entire life in Appalachia. When asked in interviews whether or not they consider themselves Appalachian, people are neither defensive nor angry; they generally shrug their shoulders and say that they have not thought about it. For this reason, we must remember that terms like *Appalachian* are purely academic descriptions and are not in the thoughts of most people under study.

In approaching a popular speech variety such as Appalachian English, the first and most difficult task is determining the object of study. The general public has clear opinions about what is and what is not Appalachian English, but for a sociolinguistic investigator, the task is much more daunting. Although ideally researchers would be able to assess Appalachian Englishes without tackling Appalachian Drawl, the stereotype is pervasive. Thus, to understand the diversity of Appalachian Englishes, we must first understand the monstrous stereotype of the Appalachian Drawl.

The Appalachian Drawl focuses on a socioregional cross section of Appalachia, namely the poorest residents of the most isolated areas of central Appalachia. Throughout the twentieth century, the media focused their attention on stereotypes from this region of Appalachia for its salability as a spectacle of human nature. Our subjects from southern West Virginia inform us that reporters from outside the region will even today search out people who fit the stereotype of the Appalachian Drawl, ignoring nine-tenths of the community; these reporters then represent the community as comprised strictly of that one-tenth.

One of the most popular examples of capitalizing on this stereotype is the comic strip Snuffy Smith. Snuffy Smith was first drawn in 1919 and is one of the longest-running cartoons in U.S. history, with syndication in twenty-one countries and eleven languages (Snuffy Smith Web site). The focus of the strip is a family of hillbillies represented much like the depiction in the first epigraph: Snuffy Smith (a "card-playin', hammock-swayin', shotgun-sprayin' varmint"), his wife Loweezy (she enjoys servin' up tasty vittles to Snuffy and the kids), and Jughaid and Tater (the young-uns). The strip relies heavily on nonstandard spelling (e.g., "propitty" for "property") and eye dialect (e.g., *yore* for *your*) to indicate the educational attainment of its characters.[1] However, these nonstandard spellings are not always just for show like eye dialect, as they often do reflect phonological variation in Appalachian or general U.S. Southern speech: In one example, *hog* is spelled as <hawg>, most likely to indicate a mid-back rounded vowel with a back upglide (i.e., [hɔ$^{w}$g]), a relatively common yet stigmatized Appalachian phonological feature. Another example of a phonological feature represented orthographically is <Jughaid> for Jug-Head, traditional slang for "a slow or stupid person" (DARE 3:172). This rendering gives an orthographic description of [ɛ] breaking to contain a front offglide [ɛ$^{y}$], a current and socially marked feature of the Southern Shift (Labov 1994; Thomas 2001; Labov, Ash, and Boberg 2002).

As television grew into the dominant communications medium in American culture, the Appalachian Drawl became the modus operandi for shows like the animated *Hillbilly Bears,* which debuted in 1965 (Hillbilly Bears Web site).[2] Hillbilly bears Maw and Paw Rugg and their two children, Floral and Shag, "are a backwoods bunch" who "react to the trials of modern life with a laid-back mountain-folk attitude—Paw mutters under his breath while Maw offers down-home insults." The added dimension over Snuffy Smith is that the Hillbilly bears have voice actors behind the characters. Paw never speaks out of a mumble, with occasional punctuations of words so that his message comes across in a telegraphic manner. Maw demonstrates a few classic Appalachian features such as /ay/-ungliding before voiceless obstruents (e.g., <right> [ra:t]) and aspects of the Southern Vowel Shift such as /ɛ/ breaking and tensing (e.g., <head> [hɛ$^{y}$d]/[hed]). Grammatical features include Scots-Irish subject-verb concord (Hazen 1996, 2000) (e.g., *Them woodpeckers is back again*) and demonstrative pronoun alternation (e.g., "those" → "them"). Other general Southern features include completive *done* (e.g., *They done raised a batch of kin-folk*) and subject relative pronoun markers, like *what* (e.g., *That's my* [ma:] *Paw what brung down that giant dragon-fly* [fla:]). Although these features certainly are contained in some of the Appalachian Englishes, for most non-Appalachians, representations of this nature are the first and most memorable source of contact and are directly linked to the "backwards" nature of such characters.

This sociolinguistic stereotype thus becomes the essence of the Appalachian Drawl, a model to which all speakers of Appalachian Englishes are compared in order to determine "authenticity." For Appalachian speakers without these traits, a common experience is to travel outside the area and have people not believe that they are from Appalachia, because the observers are quite confident that they "know" what Appalachian English sounds like.

After the 1996 Oakland School Board decision concerning Ebonics, cyberspace was flooded with derisive Ebonics humor (Ronkin and Karn 1999). As another stigmatized language variety, the Appalachian Drawl was also cyberhumored in effigy, and several circulating e-mail jokes make specific the connection between the two. The World Wide Web contains a plethora of sites devoted to "Hillbonics" or hillbilly slang, the first of which came to life in 1997. Modeled after the term Ebonics, Hillbonics is often purported to be the speech of the poorest of Appalachians. Commonly, such sites are peppered with pictures of the stereotypical ignorant hillbilly sitting in his threadbare shirt and patched bib overalls, with his jug of moonshine and gun handy, while bluegrass music plays in the background. These illustrations serve to further foster the stereotype that authentic Appalachians are poor, white, drunken, and gun-happy males. The intent of the Hillbonics sites ranges from a comical affirmation of the Appalachian Drawl stereotype to serious attempts to "chronicle this old diction." The most intricate of these pages contain lists of lexical items (e.g., gully wash: torrential rain) and phonological spellings (e.g., <far> for fire). Along with phonological and morphosyntactic features, these particular sites often include eye dialect (e.g., "whut" for "what," "yore" for "your"), a reflection of the public's perception of Appalachians as illiterate. The words themselves are frequently linked in more than one way to the public's stereotype of Appalachians as poor and backwards not only through the spelling but through the lexical contexts given (e.g., "You have some'a *yore* teeth, for which I am proud.")

The myths about Appalachian English are not always presented in a negative manner. A desire to link Appalachian people to the past is evident in many popular Appalachian Drawl myths. One popular historical myth is that Elizabethan English is still spoken in West Virginia (Montgomery 1998). This idea has been promoted by the popular literature since about 1890, especially by authors looking for "local color." Even the first dialect scholars were greatly influenced by a notion of a "Chaucerian" or "Elizabethan" speech community in Appalachia. Charles F. Smith, a member on the first editorial board of the American Dialect Society, wrote the earliest known article devoted solely to mountain speech, "On Southernisms" (1883), and he drew direct links between Elizabethan sources and mountain speech. Although the varieties of Appalachian English are diverse, Elizabethan English is not one of them. Elizabethan English, spoken during the reign of Queen Elizabeth I (1558–1603), was in fact never spoken in West Virginia. In 1603 Jamestown was only an idea, and major settlement in the region that later became West Virginia did not begin until the eighteenth century. Also, all languages change, so even if there had been a settlement of Elizabethan English speakers, and they had remained isolated until today, their great-great . . . great-grandchildren would not speak the same dialect as did their forebears. We suspect that people who promote this idea within Appalachia are trying to correct one language myth, that Appalachians speak bad English, by promoting another.

For the layperson, one of the most surprising facts about the formal study of *language* is that scholars do not have an airtight definition of the term. When scholars move to study different varieties of the same mutually intelligible version of human language, the problem of definition is thrown more strongly into relief. Popularly, Appalachian English is considered to be certain phonological, morphosyntactic, and lexical features: people expect to hear [bæ˞] for *bear* and [sodipap] for soda pop; they expect to hear phrases like *I ain't seen but one deer when we was out huntin'*. In looking to the most detailed book on Appalachian English, Wolfram and Christian (1976), we find a study of vernacular features taken from fifty-two speakers in Monroe and Mercer counties, West Virginia. This study focused on traditional language variation patterns associated with lower-socioeconomic-status communities in rural areas of southern Appalachia. The difficulty is not that the study focuses on only one geographic region, but that there are no studies of other geographic regions within Appalachia. This lack of wider sociolinguistic investigation in Appalachia contributes to a monolithic perception of Appalachian Englishes. A featural definition of Appalachian Englishes is possible, but a strict list-comparison method based on traditional variables would eliminate many, if not most, of the people living in Appalachia.

Consider that according to the Appalachian Regional Commission, Appalachia constitutes 406 counties covering 13 states—a tremendous geographic area, roughly 200,000 square miles, with a current population of about 22 million. In traveling from midstate New York to Mississippi, one encounters some substantive differences in language variation patterns, and no one, lay listener or linguist, considers speakers of these Appalachian endpoints to have the same variety of English. Even within the confines of Wolfram and Christian's designation of "Southern Appalachian Region," we have to consider language variation from Wheeling, West Virginia, to

Newnan, Georgia. Hence, within this "Southern" region appear both the Northern Cities and Southern Vowel Shifts (Labov 1994; Gordon 2001; Thomas 2001; Labov, Ash, Boberg 2002), both the low-back merger (e.g., *caught/cot*) and the *pin/pen* merger (for the former see Herold 1990; for the latter see Wise 1933; C. K. Thomas 1958; Brown 1991). A geographic delimitation of Appalachian Englishes as a coherent set of language variation patterns is not tenable. However, such a monolithic homogenization is exactly the definition most often given to English spoken in Appalachia.

The lack of geographic cohesiveness in Appalachian English is most apparent when considering the differences between urban, suburban, and rural communities. For example, growing up in southern West Virginia may or may not mean that you have Southern language variation patterns, depending on whether you grew up in suburban Charleston or in rural Logan County. Around the state capital of West Virginia, Charleston, high school students maintain strict social divisions between the suburbanites and those who live in more rural areas. These groups are divided by several socioeconomic indicators and mark their differences with their speech (Hazen and Hall 1999). The more rural *Creekers,* who live along creeks, follow Southern language variation patterns (e.g., monophthongization of /ay/); the *Hillers,* who live higher up both geographically and socioeconomically, display more Northern language variation patterns (e.g., a full off-glide with /ay/). The *Hillers* social group in the high school contains the children of professionals from other states and countries; the *Creekers* are all native-born West Virginians whose families have been in the area for at least several generations. The animosity between the two groups is in part rooted in their different orientations: the *Creekers* want to live in Appalachia, specifically the southern part, while the *Hillers* want out of their local community and Appalachia in general. Southern and non-Southern are not simply geographic areas but identities. Rural students from blue-collar families often come to high school with some Southern features that they find to be markers of peer group identity.

Social identity plays as large a role in Appalachia as it does anywhere in guiding synchronic and diachronic language variation (Hazen 2002 and cites therein), yet Appalachia lacks comprehensive identity studies. Given the difficulties in construing a unified *Appalachian English,* we feel scholars should move toward the concept of *Appalachian Englishes.* These varieties may overlap in some features, but in all likelihood, there will not be a core set of language variation patterns unique to Appalachian English.

One understudied field of research in Appalachia is ethnic variation. Although never a large percentage of the population, African Americans have been part of West Virginia and Appalachia for more than 150 years. Unfortunately, their language variation patterns have never been thoroughly documented. The vernacular English of African American Appalachians appears to blend features of both Southern AAVE and traditional rural features, for example, habitual *be* and leveled *was* (Hazen, Fluharty, and Anderson 2002; Mallinson and Wolfram 2002). AAVE also varies regionally within Appalachia. For example, West Virginia since its formation in 1863 has been divided into northern and southern cultures, a result of alliances in the Civil War. The state tends to have a sharp dialect boundary dividing it into southern and northern dialect regions (Kurath and McDavid 1961). This cultural division can also be found in African American speech. For example, /ay/ monophthongization is more frequent for African Americans in southern West Virginia. Aligned with these dialect features are many of the same cultural attitudes found in European American communities: African Americans in southern West Virginia today view themselves as both southern and African American, whereas those in northern West Virginia identify themselves as only African American.

The features labeled as Appalachian can almost all be found in older, rural varieties of European American Southern U.S. English (Labov, Ash, and Boberg 2002). Thus no features we discuss are unique to Appalachia, but these features are most often more robust in this region. Our characterizations are based on the phonological and grammatical variables investigated in Wolfram and Christian (1976). For our account, we have analyzed twenty-one of sixty-seven speakers in our sample, all of whom were born and raised in Appalachia.

For phonological variables of speakers in our sample, only five vernacular features are shared by most:

> /ay/-ungliding, e.g., *fire* /fayr/ → [faːr], *side* /sayd/ → [saːd];
>
> /ɪ/-/ɛ/ merger, e.g., *pin*/*pen* → *pin* [pɪn];
>
> /ɪ/-/i/, /ʊ/-/u/, /ɛ/-/e/ mergers, e.g., *pill* /pɪl/ → [pil];
>
> fricative stopping preceding nasals, e.g., *wasn't* /wʌznt/ → [wʌdnt];
>
> deletion of initial /ð/, e.g., *them* /ðɛm/ → [ɛm].

None of the traditional Appalachian features discussed by Wolfram and Christian (1976) are shared by everyone in the region or in our sample. The one feature that is most often socially remarked as Appalachian is one type of /ay/-ungliding, namely ungliding before voiceless obstruents (e.g., *white, rice, bike*). Although /ay/-ungliding before voiceless obstruents is certainly a feature of many Southern regions for older speakers, its rates are greatly declining for the middle-aged speakers of these regions. It is generally rare for younger Southerners outside of Appalachia and has always been extremely rare for African American communities. However, Appalachian African Americans in our sample have higher rates of /ay/-ungliding before voiceless obstruents than most African American communities, although lower than their European American counterparts.

For grammatical and lexical features of speakers in our sample, only six are extensively distributed in the speech community:

leveled *was,* e.g., *We was going over there;*

regularized past tense, e.g., *He don't have the right;*

alveolar nasal *-ing,* e.g., *I was fishing* [fɪʃɪn];

multiple negation, e.g., *I don't have no way of knowing;*

*ain't,* e.g., *I ain't scared of you;*

pleonastic pronoun, e.g., *Me and my dad, we would toss the ball.*

Although according to formal prescriptive standards all of these variables are socially stigmatized, they play a role in both middle- and working-class communities in West Virginia.

Some grammatical features of Appalachian Englishes have roots in Scots-Irish ancestry and other vernacular-speaking regions. One Scottish link is the similarity between the Appalachian mountains and the Outer Banks of North Carolina (Hazen 1996, 2000). Both settled by Scots-Irish immigrants, they share a pattern of subject-verb concord that dates back at least six centuries. This pattern includes an *-s* verb ending in sentences like *The dogs walks* and *The people goes.* The two areas also share the well-known *a*-prefixing, as in *He went a-hunting. A*-prefixing is a complex linguistic process that has undergone substantial semantic changes since its inception (Wolfram 1976, 1980; Dietrich 1981).

The majority of our features, seventeen of the twenty-four phonological variables and sixteen of the thirty-three grammatical features, are used by only our most vernacular speakers. Three of the phonological features and eleven of the grammatical features are used by none of our speakers. The variation between our speakers and those of earlier studies, plus the variation between speakers in our own sample, makes clear the need for further descriptive accounts of language variation patterns in Appalachia. At this point in the research, it is difficult to divine what social factors would best delimit Appalachian Englishes.

Taken from three different interviews, the following passages from young Appalachians illustrate the daily conflict over their varieties of English. Maggie, Lisa, and Marvin are from southern West Virginia—Logan and Mercer counties—in the heart of what has been traditionally identified as the most stereotypically Appalachian area. They reflect three different stages for young Appalachians: pre-college, college student, and college graduate. Their attitudes toward Appalachian language variation patterns do not, however, always match their production of stigmatized forms.

The most isolated of our speakers, Maggie, is fully conscious of derisive attitudes toward her language and has adopted some of these anti-Southern attitudes herself. As Lippi-Green (1997:68) argues for vernaculars of all stripes, part of the language subordination process involves vernacular speakers accepting and imposing misinformation about their vernacular at their own expense. In the following passage, Maggie reports avoiding the most marked of Southern lexical items, the second person plural, *y'all.* Maggie certainly does use *y'all* in her sociolinguistic interview, even though she derides others who use it.

[KH is the interviewer; Clara is Maggie's mother; Marge is her grandmother.]

**Maggie:** I can't stand the word *y'all,* I say *you guys.* I can't say *y'all.*

**KH:** Now you don't say *y'all,* why not?

**Maggie:** I just don't like that word.

**Clara:** I noticed her changing a little bit of what she was saying.

**KH:** Now where do you pick up *you guys* from?

**Maggie:** I just, that's what my word is. I don't say *y'all.* I can't stand it.

**Clara:** The kids now change their . . .

**KH:** When did this come in? I want to hear about this.

**Clara:** The kids do it on purpose, they change, they don't like to say *y'all.*

**Marge:** Because everybody makes fun of *you all.*

**KH:** Now Maggie, do you consider yourself southern?

**Maggie:** Yeah.

**KH:** But you don't want to use *y'all.*

**Maggie:** No. "*Y'all* come back now, ya hear."

Grammatically *y'all* is the second person plural pronominal form, for both subject and object case. As a widely recognized marker of Southern Englishes, AAVE and Appalachian English included, *y'all* is a staple of a wide variety of jokes about Southerners and is perhaps the single fastest method of characterizing a fictional persona as Southern. Maggie's mocking rendition of the clichéd farewell demonstrates the deep entrenchment of this stereotype. As a lexical item that finds a direct contrast with the second plural forms of other regional accents—*you guys* of the inland North, *you'ns* of the Pittsburgh area, *youse* of the New York/New Jersey area—*y'all* becomes a shibboleth for some and a badge of honor for others. Besides producing *y'all* in other parts of the conversation, Maggie also demonstrates several forms of an analogous first person plural pronoun form, *we-all* (e.g., *We-all call him Gator*).

Although Marvin does not demonstrate any predominantly Appalachian features and dislikes all features of any southern accent, he does have some /ay/ ungliding. As a former member of a college debate team, Marvin has spent considerable time crafting his presentation style, which we suspect was his predominant style during the sociolinguistic interview. Marvin made a choice early on to distance himself from traditional varieties of Appalachian English: "For some reason, it seems like around eighth grade or so, that it was my perception and my personal choice that I didn't want to sound like those other people." Marvin is extremely adamant in his views and is quite sure that speakers' intelligence is closely tied to their language variety: "If I go up and I talk to them, and if I sit down and automatically notice that they have, have a twang to them, or a very southern dialect, then I know that there's going to be a limit to the type of conversation that we can have . . . with the first word out of their mouth, in my mind, a door closes." Although Marvin is academically a good student, his superior grades have not helped him combat his own dialect discrimination, and he is quite aware that as a native of Southern West Virginia, he himself demonstrates how wrong the stereotype can be. But Marvin's ideas about Appalachia, like those of the American public in general, have been influenced by the popular media. He recoils from portrayals of Appalachian language varieties: "You know, if you turn on the news and there's an accident. Who is the first person that the news shows? It's, you know, it's the person with the most backward accent and it's usually typically associated with a low level of intelligence and—I know, like, I would be the first, should be the first one to discount that stereotype, but I'm not."

If identities were to be arranged in polar opposites, Lisa would be the antithesis to Marvin. A college junior who spent a summer in China for her economics studies, she is from a small southern West Virginia town. Though she intends to live and travel in other parts of the country, she is proud of both her heritage and her speech. She attends school in the more northern region of Morgantown, West Virginia, where she has crossed into a different dialect region, one heavily loaded with Northerners. Even within this socioculturally mixed environment, her Southern Appalachian features are on her mind:

**Lisa:** Yeah, it was a— it was always on my mind. It was always, if I wasn't thinking about it, someone would point it out. And I mean, I had friends who would record us and mail tapes to their family. I had a couple friends that did that, I mean, they would introduce us . . . to other people and be like, "Say *dog* [dɔg]! Say *dog* [dɔg]! Come on, say it!"

**KH:** How'd you say dog [dɔg]?

**Lisa:** Dog [dɔʷg].

Lisa's sociolinguistic interview was conducted by a professor in his office, and she remained slightly formal during the interview. However, she maintained high rates of ungliding (96%[3]) and demonstrated during a minimal pair reading list vowel mergers in the following words: *pin~pen, cot~caught, tour~tore, hill~heel, pull~pool.* She reports that some forms of her speech have changed since entering college, as she has noted in interactions with her hometown friends who had remained in southern West Virginia: "I got so much, like, my friends would be like, stop talking like that. I'm, you know, you think you're better than us, and you went off to college and now you're saying '*home*' [hõʷm] instead of '*home*' [hõʷm] . . . you know what I mean? How you, *home* [hʌ̃ʷm], instead of *home* [hõʷm]." Lisa's friends focus on part of the vowel movements in the Southern United States, often referred to as the Southern Shift (Labov 1994; Thomas 2001). As part of the Southern Shift, the back, tense, rounded vowels ([u], [o]) are fronted; for some younger speakers, these vowels are front of the mid-central vowel [ʌ] of *cut*. Maggie, Lisa's relative in southern West Virginia, is extremely advanced in all aspects of the Southern Shift, and we assume that Lisa at one point fit this norm. Lisa's friends obviously feel some kind of betrayal in the display of Lisa's non-Southern vowels (the nonfronted version of [hõʷm]). Of interest for the study of bidialectalism (Hazen 2001), Lisa first cannot produce the distinction between the Southern and non-Southern forms and comments later in the interview that it is a difficult distinction to make.

Through interactions both back in her hometown and on the culturally diverse college campus, Lisa has learned about dialect discrimination and Appalachian English: "As soon as I would open my mouth, people, I know in their head think, they judge me, they think you're dumb if you talk different. You know what I mean? I could say the same thing that someone else said, and they would think that it was unintelligent, because of the way I said it." As a result of this lesson in language politics, Lisa noted that she had to work extremely hard and strike a serious demeanor at all times during her first two years of college, especially her first semester, to compensate for other people's judgments. With dialect discrimination against certain varieties of Appalachian English enacted as a part of the college experience even within Appalachia, the stigmatization of Appalachian Englishes has reached every corner of U.S. society, even within the hearts of Appalachians themselves.

In order to better demonstrate the diversity of Appalachian Englishes and the social forces directing their flow through time, we have presented sociolinguistic characterizations of three different types:

A popular view from outside the dialect region. Although the stereotype of the Appalachian Drawl is not an accurate portrayal of what can be found in Appalachian Englishes, the wide-scale social interpretation that results from the Appalachian Drawl does affect social attitudes of synchronic variation and trends in diachronic variation.

A qualitative view of the language variation patterns to enable an accurate account of sociolinguistically diagnostic variables.

The speakers' own views of their language variety. How speakers' identities are formed in relation to their language variation patterns will influence both synchronic and diachronic variation.

As is well noted in and out of our field (Chomsky 2000:49,156), the term *dialect* is prescientific: it differs from the physics concept of an *atom* in that *dialect* has no single agreed-upon definition. As with AAVE, Appalachian English can be considered a list of features (linguistic definition) or whichever features mark its speakers as being Appalachian in some way (social definition). Thus, to define a *dialect* is both a scientific and a sociohistorical venture.

We offer a three-way analysis of Appalachian Englishes and suggest, following Rickford and Rickford (2000), that any full understanding of a dialect requires a similar tertiary view. Future studies contributing to sociolinguistic knowledge about Appalachia should include a more detailed account of inter- and intra-ethnic differences in Appalachia, including Native American Vernacular English (Dannenberg and Wolfram 1998; Dannenberg 2002), the correlation of economic trends (e.g., coal booms and busts) with diachronic language variation patterns, and ethnographic study of the identity issues surrounding the sociogeographic split between Northern and Southern culture in Appalachia.

Why do so many people feel that Appalachian English is at best "quaint" (read *useless* and *outdated*) and at worst stricken and deformed? This perception is, at its root, a social judgment of Appalachian people, not of the language they speak. Since this country's settlement, Appalachia has been perceived as backwards and exclusively poor. Although this is not a true characterization of Appalachia, even if it were true, poverty should not justify bigotry. The language judgment is nothing more than an illogical cover for an uglier prejudice.

At this point, our qualitative and quantitative research describes Appalachian Englishes that are diverse and changing. The younger southern West Virginians do not have a great many of the features, phonological or grammatical, that have been used to characterize the generations before them. From this decline of traditional Appalachian features comes not a general American homogenization of Appalachian English varieties, but language variation patterns guided by societal trends affecting the rest of the United States (such as suburbanization). However, Appalachia's unique geography still shapes its communities: In satellite images of "city lights" at night across the country ("Sprawl at Night" 2001), the outline of Appalachia is quite clear from its rural population (42% rural, as opposed to the national average of 20% [ARC]). In part because of the continuing influence of geography on Appalachian society and economy, Appalachia will continue to differentiate itself from the remainder of the United States.

The younger generation is also aware of dialect discrimination, both in themselves and in the general populace. The stereotype of the Appalachian Drawl continues to overshadow the reality of socioeconomic, ethnic, and sociogeographic diversity in Appalachian Englishes. We look forward to a developing scholarly understanding of the genuine language variation of Appalachia.

## NOTES

This research was funded through a National Science Foundation grant (BCS-9982647). Additional funding from the Department of English, the Eberly College of Arts and Sciences, and a West Virginia University Senate Research Grant (R-99-023) has also assisted this research. We would like to thank the subjects who have made their data available.

1. Eye dialect is a representation of nonstandard dialect or imputed low education level through nonstandard spellings, used even when the local pronunciation does not differ substantially from the standard.

2. Other television programs that (mis)represent Appalachians include *The Beverly Hillbillies,* which ran from 1962 to 1971, and *The Dukes of Hazard,* which ran from 1979 to 1985.

3. The 96% rate comes from 142/149 tokens of /ay/ words, which do not include the instances of *like*. Were the numbers for *like* included the rate would be 63% (152/253).

## REFERENCES

ARC. Appalachian Regional Commission. January 1997. The Appalachian Region. http://www.arc.gov/, accessed 28 March 2001.

Brown, Vivian R. 1991. Evolution of the Merger of /ɪ/ and /ɛ/ before Nasals in Tennessee. *American Speech* 66:303–15.

Chomsky, Noam. 2000. *New Horizons in the Study of Language and Mind.* Cambridge, U.K.: Cambridge University Press.

DARE. *Dictionary of American Regional English.* 1985–. Volume 2: *D–H,* ed. Frederic G. Cassidy. Volume 1: *A–D* and Volume 3: *I–O,* ed. Frederic G. Cassidy and Joan Houston Hall. Cambridge, Mass.: Belknap of Harvard University Press.

Dannenberg, Clare. 2002. *Sociolinguistic Constructs of Ethnic Identity: The Syntactic Delineation of Native American English.* Publication of the American Dialect Society, No. 87. Durham, N.C.: Duke University Press.

Dannenberg, Clare, and Walt Wolfram. 1998. Ethnic Identity and Grammatical Restructuring: Be(s) in Lumbee English. *American Speech* 73:1–21.

Dietrich, Julia C. 1981. The Gaelic Roots of *A*-prefixing in Appalachian English. *American Speech* 56:314.

Gordon, Matthew. 2001. *Small-Town Values and Big-City Vowels : A Study of the Northern Cities Shift in Michigan*. Publication of the American Dialect Society, No. 84. Durham, N.C.: Duke University Press.

Hazen, Kirk. 1996. Dialect Affinity and Subject-Verb Concord: The Appalachian–Outer Banks Connection. *SECOL Review* 20:25–53.

———. 2000. Subject-Verb Concord in a Post-insular Dialect: The Gradual Persistence of Dialect Patterning. *Journal of English Linguistics* 28:127–44.

———. 2001. *An Introductory Investigation into Bidialectalism*. University of Pennsylvania Working Papers in Linguistics, Volume 7.3. Selected Papers from NWAV 29. Philadelphia: University of Pennsylvania Press.

———. 2002. Identity and Language Variation in a Rural Community. *Language* 78:240–57.

Hazen, Kirk, Ellen Fluharty, and Ilana Anderson. 2002. African American Appalachian English. MS. West Virginia Dialect Project, Morgantown, W.V.

Hazen, Kirk, and Ellen Fluharty. 2001. Defining Appalachian English. *American Language Review* May/June 5(3):32–33.

Hazen, Kirk, and Laine Hall. 1999. Dialect Shifts in West Virginia Families. Paper presented at Southeastern Conference on Linguistics 60. Norfolk, Va.

Herold, Ruth. 1990. Mechanisms of Merger: The Implementation and Distribution of the Low Back Merger in Eastern Pennsylvania. Ph.D. dissertation, University of Pennsylvania.

Hillbilly Bears Web site. Formerly at http://www.cartoonnetwork.com/doc/hillbilly_bears/, accessed 2002.

Kurath, Hans, and Raven I. McDavid Jr. 1961. *The Pronunciation of English in the Atlantic States*. Ann Arbor: University of Michigan Press.

Labov, William. 1994. *Principles of Linguistic Change: Internal Factors*. Cambridge, Mass.: Basil Blackwell.

Labov, William, Sharon Ash, and Charles Boberg. 2002. *The Atlas of North American English*. http://www.ling.upenn.edu/phono_atlas/, accessed 16 June 2003.

Lippi-Green, Rosina. 1997. *English with an Accent: Language, Ideology, and Discrimination in the United States*. London: Routledge.

Mallinson, Christine, and Walt Wolfram. 2002. Dialect Accommodation in a Bi-ethnic Mountain Enclave Community: More Evidence on the Development of African American Vernacular English. *Language in Society* 31:743–75.

Montgomery, Michael. 1998. In the Appalachians They Speak like Shakespeare. In *Language Myths*, ed. Laurie Bauer and Peter Trudgill, pp. 66–76. New York: Penguin.

Rickford, John, and Russell Rickford. 2000. *Spoken Soul: The Story of Black English*. New York: Wiley and Sons.

Ronkin, Maggie, and Helen Karn. 1999. Mock Ebonics: Linguistic Racism in Parodies of Ebonics on the Internet. *Journal of Sociolinguistics*. 3(3):360–80.

Smith, C. F. 1883. On Southernisms. *Transactions of the American Philological Society*. 14:42–56.

Snuffy Smith Web site. http://www.kingfeatures.com/features/comics/bgoogle/about.htm, accessed 16 June 2003.

"Sprawl at Night: Seeing the Light." *National Geographic Magazine*. July 2001: 57. http://www.nationalgeographic.com/.

Thomas, Charles Kenneth. 1958. *An Introduction to the Phonetics of American English*. New York: Ronald.

Thomas, Erik R. 2001. *An Acoustic Analysis of Vowel Variation in New World English*. Publication of the American Dialect Society, No. 85. Durham, N.C.: Duke University Press.

Wise, Claude Merton. 1933. Southern American Dialect. *American Speech*. 8(2): 37–43.

Wolfram, Walt. 1976. Toward a Description of "A"-prefixing in Appalachian English. *American Speech* 51:45–56.

Wolfram, Walt. 1980. "A"-prefixing in Appalachian English. In *Locating Language in Time and Space,* ed. William Labov, pp. 107–42. New York: Academic.

Wolfram, Walt, and Donna Christian. 1976. *Appalachian Speech*. Washington, D.C.: Center for Applied Linguistics.

# Constructing Ethnolinguistic Groups: A Sociolinguistic Case Study

*Christine Mallinson*

Sociolinguistic studies of African American Vernacular English (AAVE) have long been predicated on a dichotomous categorization of the speech of African Americans and European Americans. This dichotomy has played a particular role in hypotheses about the historical development of AAVE. For example, one of the major theories about AAVE's development—the so-called divergence theory, which postulates that African American Vernacular English and Earlier African American Vernacular English were once similar but have since become dissimilar (Labov 1985; Bailey & Maynor 1987, 1989)—is based on the assumption that the speakers who are identified as African Americans and European Americans constitute discrete groups.

But given current social circumstances in the United States, in which Americans of color have a range of options to choose from when deciding how to construct and present their ethnic identity (Song 2001), this traditional premise may no longer be appropriate. As the situation in Beech Bottom—an isolated, nonwhite Appalachian community in North Carolina—illustrates, attempting to classify sociolinguistic informants based on a binary black/white conception of ethnicity can be complicated. In this community, older residents, who self-identify as African American, exhibit dialect patterns more typical of African American English. In contrast, the speech of the younger residents, who self-identify as multiethnic, nearly matches the dialect of their European American cohorts, particularly in their Appalachian phonology and in their lack of traditional African American English grammatical and phonological features. This research investigates variation in the accommodation of the speech of the Beech Bottom residents to the dialect of their local cohort European Americans. As the data reveal, there are risks inherent in creating predetermined and artificial groups of informants that imply discrete sociolinguistic and ethnic boundaries, as different linguistic options may be available to informants in the process of their dialect accommodation, depending on their ethnic self-identification.

## SOCIOHISTORICAL CONTEXT OF AN ISOLATED COMMUNITY

The receding mountain community of Beech Bottom is located in Avery County, North Carolina, about thirty-five miles southwest of Boone along the Tennessee border. Beech Bottom lies within the southeastern region of Appalachia, as defined by the Appalachian Regional Commission (2000). Appalachia is a region that has not always been recognized for its diversity (Billings 1989), but the actual history of Appalachia contradicts longstanding stereotypes about the region's homogeneity. Native American influence in the region has historically been strong, the ancestry of European settlers in Appalachia was quite varied (Beaver and Lewis 1998), and African Americans slaves were brought to Appalachia as early as the mid–seventeenth century (Kay and Cary 1995). As Ostwalt and Pollitt (2001:235), who studied the Salem School and Orphanage for African Americans (located about ten miles from Beech Bottom), summarize, "The myth persists that the Appalachian region is a static and uniform society made up of poor white mountaineers. But the social and cultural makeup of the region is much more complicated than some are willing to admit."

Just as Appalachia more generally was settled by diverse groups of people, so too was Avery County. Around 1780, Colonel Waightsill Avery, for whom Avery County was eventually named, settled in the area with his African American slaves. After slavery was abolished, Avery gave his freed slaves a large tract of land that lies about a half-mile from Beech Bottom (Ollis 2002). Though information is sparse, it seems probable that Avery's former slaves were the ancestors of some of today's Beech Bottom residents. There were other settlers as well; local history maintains that Beech Bottom was formally settled in 1850 by a man named Hampton Jackson (Harris 1994; Joslin 1995). Although Jackson's own ethnicity is not recorded, he raised two adopted sons, one of Native American and Polish descent and the other of Native American and German descent.

As its population grew, Beech Bottom developed as a multiethnic community. Between 1900 and 1940, it ranged from 80 to 111 people and included residents of African American, European American, and Native American descent (Harris 1994). In fact, during this period, nonwhites in Beech Bottom outnumbered whites 65 to 46 (Harris 1994; Joslin 1995). Historically, Beech Bottom's primary industry was feldspar mining, but as the mines began to close in the early 1940s, residents migrated north to seek work. The mobilizing effects of World War II also took a toll on the community's population as some locals who had joined the service resettled elsewhere upon their return. Christmas tree farming is now Beech Bottom's primary industry. Two farms with a total of approximately one hundred thousand trees employ two residents full-time, and other residents tend or sell trees on a part-time basis.

Currently, only about seven longtime nonwhite residents live in Beech Bottom. While Beech Bottom's older residents consistently identify as "black," the community's younger residents self-identify as multiethnic (Harris 1994; Joslin 1995), and they herald Beech Bottom's legacy as a multiethnic community. In fact, all of the nonwhite residents we interviewed preferred to minimize talk about ethnic divisions between whites and blacks and instead described their community as multicultural and racially harmonious. Despite this picture of harmony and integration, however, *post facto* segregation still exists in the community. In a prime example, about seven nonwhite residents regularly attend the Beech Bottom Mennonite Brethren church, but no European Americans do. A strict racial boundary is also implied in the ways that the nonwhite Beech Bottom residents are classified by the European Americans. As one older European American male put it,

> Well, see, there's white people and then they say colored people here. [laughter] I didn't say the wrong word there. [more laughter] Beech Bottoms was where they lived, the colored people . . . And that's the only place they settled.

Regardless of how the nonwhite residents self-identify, a conception of the community as multiethnic is counterbalanced by the historical reality of race relations within the American South and the corresponding fundamental biethnic dichotomy that still exists and that demarcates the African American and European American communities in Beech Bottom. According to Nagel (1994:156), this is a common situation for blacks in the United States: "While blacks may make intra-racial distinctions based on ancestry or skin tone, the power of race as a socially defining status in U.S. society makes these internal differences rather unimportant in interracial settings in comparison to the fundamental black/white color boundary."

This complex racial and ethnic situation naturally raises several questions for researchers. For example, how should we label the nonwhite Beech Bottom residents—can they all be classified as African American? If not, what factors should be taken into account? And for those residents who identify as multiethnic, is this self-identification manifested linguistically? To begin to answer these questions and to try to sort out possible relationships between dialect and ethnic self-identification, I and other fieldworkers interviewed several lifetime residents of both Beech Bottom and a neighboring white community. I then grouped informants along traditional binary ethnic lines—labeling the Beech Bottom residents "African Americans" and the white residents "European Americans"—as a basis for examining a set of regionally and ethnically sensitive linguistic variables.

In the linguistic analysis, data from the interviews of three African American male speakers—ages 72, 39, and 13 at the time of interview—are considered. (No African American women were included in the analysis because of inadequate sample size.) The analysis also includes data from the interviews of nine European American speakers: five men, ages 89, 79, 65, 55, and 35 when interviewed, and four women, ages 72, 70, 31 and 25. Most of the individuals were interviewed on more than one occasion. The combined interviews yielded approximately fifteen hours of relatively natural, recorded conversation from which to extract data.

## LINGUISTIC ANALYSIS

This study analyzes four linguistic variables, all of which are well documented regional and/or ethnic variables of American English and therefore provide a comparable database for examining ethnic alignment in biethnic enclave communities (Wolfram and Schilling-Estes 1998). Two morphosyntactic variables are analyzed: third person plural *-s* attachment, as in *The dogs barks;* and third person singular *-s* absence, as in *The dog bark.* Two phonological variables are also analyzed: syllable-coda consonant cluster reduction, as in *wes'* for *west;* and /ai/ glide reduction, as in [taːm] for *time.* While third person plural *-s* attachment and /ai/ glide reduction are strongly associated with Appalachian speech (Wolfram and Christian 1976; Christian, Wolfram, and Dube 1988; Montgomery and Hall 2002), third person singular *-s* absence and consonant cluster reduction are associated with AAVE (Labov, Cohen, Robins, and Lewis 1968; Wolfram 1969; Fasold 1972; Bailey and Thomas 1998; Rickford 1999). The range of variables in-

Table 1 Incidence of third person plural *-s* attachment by generation and ethnicity

| Speaker group | 3rd pl. *-s* attachment/total | % attached |
|---|---|---|
| Beech Bottom African Americans (N = 3) | | |
| Older (age = 72) | 12/43 | 27.9% |
| Middle (age = 39) | 8/66 | 12.1% |
| Younger (age = 13) | 0/11 | 0.0% |
| TOTAL | 20/120 | 16.7% |
| Local cohort European Americans (N = 9) | | |
| Older (ages 55+) | 16/76 | 21.1% |
| Younger (35 and under) | 22/103 | 21.4% |
| TOTAL | 38/179 | 21.2% |

cludes both Appalachian and AAVE structures so that we may assess dialect accommodation and alignment.

### *Morphosyntactic Variables*

The first variable to be examined is third person plural *-s* attachment. This concord pattern, in which *-s* is marked on a verb with a plural subject, as in *People goes there,* is widely documented as a feature of American English varieties that were influenced by Ulster Scots, which includes Appalachian English (Wolfram and Christian 1976; Christian et al. 1988; Montgomery 1989). By contrast, this feature is not typical of subject-verb concord in AAVE (Labov et al. 1968; Fasold and Wolfram 1970; Fasold 1972; Rickford 1999). Table 1 gives the figures for the overall incidence of *-s* attachment with third person plural subjects for the African American and European American speakers in the Beech Bottom sample. As table 1 shows, their rates for this feature are quite similar (approximately 17% and 21%), and results from a Chi square test that compared the rates for the two ethnic groups confirmed that there was no statistical significance to the difference.

That the Beech Bottom African Americans attach third person plural *-s* at all suggests that they are sensitive to the dialect norms characteristic of the

Table 2 Incidence of third person singular *-s* absence by generation and ethnicity

| Speaker group | 3rd sg. *-s* absence/total | % absent |
|---|---|---|
| Beech Bottom African Americans | | |
| Older | 17/57 | 29.8% |
| Middle | 15/63 | 23.8% |
| Younger | 0/21 | 0.0% |
| TOTAL | 32/141 | 22.7% |
| Local cohort European Americans | | |
| Older | 2/96 | 2.1% |
| Younger | 1/75 | 1.3% |
| TOTAL | 3/171 | 1.8% |

regional vernacular. At the same time, the data indicate that the youngest nonwhite speaker does not accommodate to this traditional Appalachian morphosyntactic variable, as the older or middle-aged African Americans do. In other words, although the African Americans and the European Americans as groups do not appear to differ in terms of this feature, when we separate the data by age as well, the youngest nonwhite speaker is differentiated from the other African Americans.

A second dimension of subject-verb concord is the optional attachment of *-s* to third person singular verbs, as in *The dog bark.* This variable is well documented in AAVE throughout the United States (Labov et al. 1968; Wolfram 1969; Fasold and Wolfram 1970; Fasold 1972; Labov 1972; Winford 1998; Rickford 1999). In contrast, third person singular *-s* absence rarely surfaces in Appalachian English (Fasold 1972; Wolfram and Fasold 1974; Wolfram and Christian 1976). Table 2 shows the figures for the African American and European American speakers in this corpus, with the overall incidence and the breakdown by age.

The data on third person singular *-s* absence for African Americans and European Americans as groups reflect a pattern of ethnic differentiation, as would be expected. As a whole, the European American speakers have an extremely low rate of third person singular *-s* absence (less than 2%), while the African Americans exhibit a rate of almost 23%. A Chi square test showed that the statistical difference between the African Americans' rates and those of the European Americans is highly significant (total $X^2 = 34.01$; df = 1; $p < .001$). Still, the difference between the two ethnic groups is due mostly to the oldest speaker's rates of third person singular *-s* absence. Additionally, there are no tokens of third person singular *-s* absence in the speech of the youngest Beech Bottom African American, which suggests an erosion of an ethnolinguistic marker and a movement toward greater assimilation to the European American cohort variety.

An analysis of the two morphological variables, third person plural *-s* attachment and third person singular *-s* absence, reveals different patterns of dialect accommodation and ethnolinguistic boundary maintenance for the Beech Bottom African Americans. Although one might expect to find all three speakers showing similar usage rates for third person singular *-s* absence, which is a highly salient African American English feature, the young African American speaker did not exhibit this feature at all in our sample. For the traditional Appalachian English variable of third person plural *-s* attachment, the young African American shows reduced usage rates for this feature compared to both the other African American speakers and the European American speakers. Thus the data indicate that the youngest African American resident deviates drastically from the dialect patterns of the other two African American speakers, who are quite vernacular and who use morphological features typical both of AAVE and of Appalachian English in their speech.

### *Phonological Variables*

The first of the two phonological variables I considered is syllable-coda consonant cluster reduction. The reduction of syllable-coda consonant clusters that share the feature of voicing (e.g., *cold* but not *colt*) is a highly diagnostic ethnolinguistic marker in American English (see, for example, Labov et al. 1968; Wolfram 1969; Fasold 1972; Guy 1980; Wolfram, Childs, and Torbert 2000). Unlike European American vernacular varieties, AAVE varieties tend to have extensive prevocalic cluster reduction—for example, speakers of AAVE would tend to say *wes' end* instead of *west end*. Table 3 provides figures for monomorphemic (e.g., *mist*) and bimorphemic (e.g., *missed*) syllable-coda cluster reduction for the Beech Bottom African Americans and their local cohort European Americans. As the data show, the African Americans' rates for this feature are well above the European Americans', though the difference in the pronunciation of the bimorphemic

Table 3 Incidence of prevocalic consonant cluster reduction by generation, ethnicity, and cluster type

| Speaker group | Prevocalic reduction/total, monomorphemic (e.g., mist) | % reduced | Prevocalic reduction/total, bimorphemic (e.g., missed) | % reduced |
|---|---|---|---|---|
| Beech Bottom African Americans | | | | |
| Older | 11/30 | 36.6% | 5/35 | 14.3% |
| Middle | 2/16 | 12.5% | 2/17 | 11.8% |
| Younger | 2/8 | 25.0% | 1/20 | 5.0% |
| TOTAL | 15/54 | 27.8% | 8/72 | 11.1% |
| Local cohort European Americans | | | | |
| Older | 2/38 | 5.3% | 3/55 | 5.4% |
| Younger | 0/12 | 0.0% | 1/14 | 7.1% |
| TOTAL | 2/50 | 5.0% | 4/69 | 5.8% |

term is due mainly to the older speakers' rates of reduction. Interestingly, the youngest nonwhite resident's rate of reduction in the bimorphemic sample is similar to that of his white cohorts.

The second phonological variable I considered is the /ai/ glide, which may be reduced or monophthongized to [a] in many varieties of Southern English. In Appalachian English, as documented by Hall (1942), Wolfram and Christian (1976), and Hazen and Fluharty (2001), speakers reduce /ai/ regardless of whether the following environment is voiceless (e.g., *tight*), voiced (e.g., *tide*), or in open syllables (e.g., *bye*). Other Southern varieties—African American English included—reduce /ai/ only before voiced segments and in open syllables (Kurath and McDavid 1961; Wolfram and Fasold 1974; Wolfram 1994; Bailey and Thomas 1998). Therefore, the incidence of prevoiceless ungliding should be diagnostic of accommodation to the regional version of /ai/ ungliding.

Table 4 gives the incidence of /ai/ ungliding in prevoiced and prevoiceless contexts for the Beech Bottom African Americans and their European American cohorts. As the data reveal, both European American and African American speakers reduce the /ai/ glide near-categorically in all environments. Though recent studies have shown that other African American

Table 4 Incidence of /ai/ ungliding

| Speaker group | Ungliding prevoiceless/ total | % unglided | Ungliding prevoiced/ total | % unglided |
|---|---|---|---|---|
| Beech Bottom African Americans | | | | |
| Older | 83/86 | 96.5% | 51/51 | 100.0% |
| Middle | 40/40 | 100.0% | 36/37 | 97.3% |
| Younger | 24/24 | 100.0% | 27/27 | 100.0% |
| TOTAL | 147/150 | 98.0% | 114/115 | 99.1% |
| Local cohort European Americans | | | | |
| Older | 106/107 | 99.1% | 118/118 | 100.0% |
| Younger | 69/69 | 100.0% | 50/50 | 100.0% |
| TOTAL | 175/176 | 99.4% | 168/168 | 100.0% |

populations may exhibit prevoiceless ungliding to some extent (Hazen and Fluharty 2001; Anderson 2002), none of them comes close to showing the near-categorical levels of ungliding found in Beech Bottom. This community's uniqueness is probably due to its insularity and the general intensity of vernacular structures manifested by these speakers. For this reason, the level of alignment between African Americans and European Americans for this feature is noteworthy: the speech of the Beech Bottom African Americans and that of their European American cohorts have basically converged to the point of being indistinguishable with respect to /ai/ ungliding.

The results obtained from analyzing these two phonological variables of prevocalic syllable-coda consonant cluster reduction and prevoiceless /ai/ ungliding at first seem to be disparate: because the Beech Bottom African Americans show almost complete accommodation to the European American dialect in their near-total /ai/ ungliding, yet they also show a clear ethnolinguistic division by maintaining relatively elevated levels of cluster reduction. Both of these features are dialect markers of Appalachian English and AAVE, respectively, but is one more salient than the other? In other words, how is the dialect of the Beech Bottom African Americans perceived by outsiders?

In the search for a partial answer to this question, I constructed a simple perception test and gave it to a group of students at North Carolina State University (Mallinson 2002). In this perception test, twenty-to-thirty-second passages of nine speakers' conversations were played for respondents. Speakers varied by age, sex, ethnicity, and place of residency in North Carolina, and listeners were asked to identify each speaker's age, ethnicity, and sex. Included in the test were passages from the interviews of the older and middle-aged African Americans and one European American male from Beech Bottom. Results from the perception test were unequivocal: listeners assumed that the African American Beech Bottom residents were European American. Whereas respondents correctly identified the ethnicity of the European American male at rates of over 90%, they misidentified the two Beech Bottom African American speakers as white more than 90% of the time.

Thus, despite a persistent ethnolinguistic divide, most outside listeners perceive the African American Beech Bottom residents to be European American. The reason for such extensive misidentification may lie in the kinds of similarities and differences between African Americans and European Americans in the region. Most prominently, these African Americans share a common regional vowel system with their European American neighbors. It is possible, then, that regional vowels are a strong determinant in judgments of ethnicity, and that their perceptual saliency might obscure other variables in the identification of speaker ethnicity.

## CONCLUSIONS

What can we conclude about the ethnolinguistic history of Beech Bottom in particular and the trajectory of change in African American Vernacular English in general? First, it is undeniable that the Beech Bottom African Americans have accommodated their dialect to the norms of Appalachian English—for the older and middle-aged residents, to the morphosyntactic variable of third person plural *-s* attachment, and for all residents, to the phonological norm of prevoiceless /ai/ ungliding—which no doubt contributes to the perception that they sound "white." At the same time, however, a detailed linguistic analysis reveals that the older and middle-aged Beech Bottom residents have significant levels of variables typical of African American Vernacular English. These patterns and the resulting ethnolinguistic divide subtly differentiate the speech of the older and middle-aged African Americans from that of their local European American cohorts.

In the speech of the youngest nonwhite resident, however, few traces of any dialect patterns typical of African American English remain. For example, instead of preserving subtle levels of third person singular *-s* absence in his dialect as the older and middle-aged Beech Bottom residents have done, the teenager's speech more closely approximates the dialect of his white cohorts in terms of this feature. This finding contradicts data from investigations of other rural communities in North Carolina (Wolfram, Thomas, and Green 2000; Wolfram and Thomas 2002), which show strong evidence that the speech of middle-aged and younger African Americans is changing in the direction of an external, transregional norm of African American English. So what might explain the near-total dialect accommodation of this young resident?

To begin with, we know that certain features characteristic of African American Vernacular English are most evident in the speech of the oldest African American, who grew up in the days of segregation, when the biracial taxonomy of the American South was still the norm and when all nonwhites were considered black or colored, regardless of how they preferred to identify themselves. For the middle-aged speaker, this ethnolinguistic boundary has begun to erode. During the time of his dialect formation, the South was experiencing desegregation. The dissolution of the prevailing patterns of racial segregation allowed new racial and ethnic taxonomies to emerge, and nonwhite individuals began to develop an ethnic consciousness—as is fully realized in the youngest nonwhite resident. Unlike the older members of his community, this young man self-identifies as multiethnic and accommodates his dialect much less to norms of African American English than to the local, stereotypically European American vernacular.

Several major factors may have combined to accelerate the process of dialect accommodation for the youngest nonwhite Beech Bottom resident. First is the fact that he lives in a community in transition, where drastic outmigration has changed the characteristics of the population considerably. Second, this resident's experience of growing up nonwhite in Beech Bottom was probably quite different from that of the other members of his community. Whereas they experienced institutional segregation and racial tension, he grew up in a society where present-day social circumstances allow for pride in ethnic heritage and the power to dispute categorical and imprecise definitions of race or ethnicity (Nagel 1994; Song 2001). Finally, the historical and current isolation of the few remaining African Americans in Beech Bottom has perhaps precluded the development of a strong black youth culture in the community. Most of this young speaker's peers are white, and as he is not yet old enough to join the military or travel extensively on his own, his contact with young African Americans is severely limited. Thus, a converging cultural milieu combined with a multiethnic self-identification may have facilitated a more pronounced movement toward the regional dialect norm in the speech of this youngest nonwhite resident, while traces of a distinctive ethnolinguistic past continue to erode.

To summarize, the Beech Bottom situation illustrates the different linguistic options that may be available to isolated African American communities in their dialect development. The evidence from the youngest Beech Bottom speaker in particular suggests that we must not assume that previously persistent dialect boundaries will necessarily hold over time for all residents of a community. Further research should be done to determine other ways in which nonwhite individuals in similar communities may restructure their linguistic identity. More generally, however, we have seen in Beech Bottom a situation in which traditional, binary conceptions of ethnicity do not hold for all speakers. Although grouping informants on the basis of presumed social characteristics may yield interesting correlates, patterns of sociolinguistic variation may be more complex. I would therefore caution that sociolinguists should not group their informants using predetermined ethnic classifications, since ethnicity—like all social constructs—is fluid and negotiated.

## NOTES

The author gratefully acknowledges the support of the William C. Friday Endowment at North Carolina State University for funding this research. Special thanks to Walt Wolfram, Dani Schreier, Karen Lavarello Schreier, and Jaclyn Fried for their contributions to this research and to the residents of Beech Bottom for their participation.

## REFERENCES

Anderson, Bridget L. 2002. Dialect Leveling and /ai/ Monophthongization among African American Detroiters. *Journal of Sociolinguistics* 6:86–98.

Appalachian Regional Commission. 2000. The Appalachian Region. http://www.arc.gov/, accessed 17 June 2003.

Bailey, Guy, and Natalie Maynor. 1987. Decreolization? *Language in Society* 16: 449–74.

———. 1989. The Divergence Controversy. *American Speech* 64:12–39.

Bailey, Guy, and Erik R. Thomas. 1998. Some Aspects of African American Vernacular English Phonology. In *African American English: Structure, History, and Use,* ed. Salikoko Mufwene, John R. Rickford, Guy Bailey, and John Baugh, pp. 85–109. London: Routledge.

Beaver, Patricia D., and Helen M. Lewis. 1998. Uncovering the Trail of Ethnic Denial: Ethnicity in Appalachia. In *Cultural Diversity in the U.S. South: Anthropological Contributions to a Region in Transition,* ed. Carole E. Hill and Patricia D. Beaver, pp. 52–68. Athens: University of Georgia Press.

Billings, Dwight B. 1989. Appalachians. In *Encyclopedia of Southern Culture,* ed. Charles Reagan Wilson and William Ferris, pp. 418. Chapel Hill: University of North Carolina Press.

Christian, Donna, Walt Wolfram, and Nanjo Dube. 1988. *Variation and Change in Geographically Isolated Communities: Appalachian and Ozark English.* Publication of the American Dialect Society, No. 74. Tuscaloosa: University of Alabama Press.

Fasold, Ralph W. 1972. *Tense Marking in Black English: A Linguistic and Social Analysis*. Washington, D.C.: Center for Applied Linguistics.

Fasold, Ralph W., and Walt Wolfram. 1970. Some Linguistic Features of Negro Dialect. In *Teaching Standard English in the Inner City,* ed. Ralph W. Fasold and Roger W. Shuy, pp. 41–86. Washington, D.C.: Center for Applied Linguistics.

Guy, Gregory R. 1980. Variation in the Group and the Individual: The Case of Final Stop Deletion. In *Locating Language in Time and Space,* ed. William Labov, pp. 1–36. New York: Academic.

Hall, Joseph S. 1942. *The Phonetics of Great Smoky Mountain Speech*. Ph.D. Dissertation, Columbia University, New York.

Harris, Jeffery. 1994. Does Beech Bottoms Still Exist? Lees McCrae College Senior Thesis.

Hazen, Kirk, and Ellen Fluharty. 2001. Defining Appalachian English: West Virginia and Beyond. Paper delivered at the Annual Meeting on New Ways of Analyzing Variation, Raleigh, N.C.

Joslin, Michael. 1995. Rooted in Harmony. *The Multi-Cultural Digest* (Asheville), July 7.

Kay, Marvin L., and Lorin Lee Cary. 1995. *Slavery in North Carolina, 1748–1775.* Chapel Hill: University of North Carolina Press.

Kurath, Hans, and Raven I. McDavid Jr. 1961. The Pronunciation of English in the Atlantic States. Ann Arbor: University of Michigan Press.

Labov, William. 1972. *Language in the Inner City: Studies in the Black English Vernacular.* Philadelphia: University of Pennsylvania Press.

——— . 1985. The Increasing Divergence of Black and White Vernaculars: Introduction to the Research Reports. MS. University of Pennsylvania, Philadelphia.

Labov, William, Paul Cohen, Clarence Robins, and John Lewis. 1968. *A Study of the Non-standard English of Negro and Puerto-Rican Speakers in New York City.* U.S. Office of Education, Final Report, Research Project 3288.

Mallinson, Christine. 2002. *The Regional Accommodation of African American English: Evidence from a Bi-ethnic Mountain Enclave Community.* M.A. thesis, North Carolina State University, Raleigh.

Montgomery, Michael. 1989. The Roots of Appalachian English. *English World-Wide* 10:227–78.

Montgomery, Michael, and Joseph Hall. 2002. *Dictionary of Smoky Mountain English.* Knoxville: University of Tennessee Press.

Nagel, Joane. 1994. Constructing Ethnicity: Creating and Recreating Ethnic Identity and Culture. *Social Problems* 41:152–76.

Ollis, Baxter. 2002. The Men and Women of Avery County. http://freepages.genealogy.rootsweb.com/~ollis/BOSTONOLLISES/furthernotesbostonhistory.html, accessed 17 June 2003.

Ostwalt, Conrad, and Phoebe Pollitt. 2001. The Salem School and Orphanage: White Missionaries, Black School. In *Appalachians and Race: The Mountain South from Slavery to Segregation,* ed. John C. Inscoe, pp. 235–44. Lexington: University Press of Kentucky.

Rickford, John R. 1999. *African American Vernacular English: Features, Evolution, Educational Implications.* Malden, Mass.: Blackwell.

Song, Miri. 2001. Comparing Minorities' Ethnic Options. *Ethnicities* 1:57–82.

Winford, Donald. 1998. On the Origins of African American Vernacular English—A Creolist Perspective, Part II: The Features. *Diachronica* 15:99–154.

Wolfram, Walt. 1969. *A Sociolinguistic Description of Detroit Negro Speech.* Washington, D.C.: Center for Applied Linguistics.

———. 1994. The Phonology of a Sociocultural Variety: The Case of African American Vernacular English. In *Child Phonology: Characteristics, Assessment, and Intervention with Special Populations,* ed. John Bernthal and Nicholas Bankston, pp. 227–44. New York: Thieme.

Wolfram, Walt, and Donna Christian. 1976. *Appalachian English.* Washington, D.C.: Center for Applied Linguistics.

Wolfram, Walt, and Ralph W. Fasold. 1974. *The Study of Social Dialects in American English.* Englewood Cliffs, N.J.: Prentice-Hall.

Wolfram, Walt, and Natalie Schilling-Estes. 1998. *American English.* Malden, Mass.: Blackwell.

Wolfram, Walt, and Erik R. Thomas. 2002. *The Development of African American English.* Malden, Mass.: Blackwell.

Wolfram, Walt, Becky Childs, and Benjamin Torbert. 2000. Tracing Language History through Consonant Cluster Reduction. *Southern Journal of Linguistics* 24:17–40.

Wolfram, Walt, Erik R. Thomas, and Elaine W. Green. 2000. The Regional Context of Earlier African American Speech: Evidence for Reconstructing the Development of AAVE. *Language in Society* 29:315–55.

# Language and Culture Pullout Program: Seminole Initiatives to Preserve Language

*Susan E. Stans and Louise Gopher*

*Ponce, este-cate, este-luste, sofkee, chickee, cufe, eco,* colors, numbers and a few memorized songs. Those are among the few Native Creek words our children know. Only a few of our children in the Seminole Tribe of Florida are apt to use Creek words with their peers, and those words are inserted into English sentences. Some words are from Mikasuki, a separate but related language. We could probably easily count all they know. Sadly, their parents cannot speak Creek to teach them. Some parents may be passive speakers, understanding much of what they hear their elders speak, but not able to converse in Creek. English is used as a *lingua franca* in conducting business and tribal government because our tribe has two native languages—Creek and Mikasuki. Bilingual friends and co-workers occasionally use Creek in conversation, but not frequently. Most of those under the age of fifty do not know the names for medicinal plants.

Our language is Creek, known as Muskogee in Oklahoma. Our language is different enough that we resist using Oklahoma Creek teaching materials. No new words are being formed in our language. If we wanted to speak our language, we would have to use many English words to talk about today's technology and ideas. The speakers who know the most words, stories, tenses, and language structure are becoming old and infirm. Our pool of experts on our language is dying with our elders. And yet we disagree among ourselves about whose pronunciation is correct. We have avoided the help of outsiders because we consider our language our exclusive right to know. Many individuals consider writing our language to be taboo because it is not our "traditional way." Others simply don't want to write the language; they just want to speak it. Our college-bound children take Spanish or Latin to fulfill their requirement for a language. After collecting data on speakers and passive speakers, linguist Tom Sawallis has estimated that by 2050 the last Creek speakers in Florida will die, taking the language with them if no more opportunities for Creek acquisition exist.

What does all this mean to us? How do we motivate children and adults to work to revive our language? How do we explain to nonspeakers what it means to us personally and as a culture?

How serious is the problem? Michael Krauss, director of the Native Language Center (Shorris 2000:35–36), estimates that only 20 of the 175 native languages spoken in the United States will survive much longer. Creek as it is known in Florida is endangered because of the small body of speakers there and the exclusive use of English in schools, the English media, marrying out among English speakers, and the lack of opportunity to hear Creek occurring naturally in daily life.

Brighton Reservation near Okeechobee, Florida, has been the home for the Florida Creek language. There are approximately 450 Seminoles living there. Children attend local public or private schools. About 50% of a random sample of the adult community spoke English only in a 1995 survey (Stans 1996:47). The other half spoke English and Creek, or English and Mikasuki, or all three. Some of our elders speak no English. No children from third through twelfth grade speak Creek. An important link to learning and enculturation of our ways has been broken.

We should make an effort to keep our language because we have only one generation of active speakers left to teach our children.

Although language loss has crept into our community, we have shown increasing interest in rescuing the Creek language as an important element in Seminole identity and culture. In the last eight years new initiatives have taken place: a ten-week adult Creek class; culture and language staff attending conferences and workshops on teaching and language; the formation of a language committee; the hiring of a linguist to create a Florida Creek dictionary; participation in summer workshops with William and Mary linguist Jack Martin and University of Oklahoma Creek teacher Margaret Mauldin; attending anthropological linguistics classes at Florida Gulf Coast University; teaching elementary children twice a week in the Okeechobee public school system; emphasis on language use and speech in the reservation prekindergarten program; using the language in print; recording fluent speakers on video- and audiotapes; and finally developing a language staff with the determination and literacy skills to promote language use. It is within this background of increased activity and more frequent language discussions that a pullout program is being planned to teach the language.

## THE PULLOUT PROGRAM IDEA

Two young adults who do not speak the language got the program started. A young mom, Rita Gopher, first came up with the idea. While in high school, Rita was in the gifted program, which pulled her from regular classes for a full day of special activities once a week. Several years later, when several of us were sitting and talking, the conversation turned to language and culture as it frequently did. We were probably thinking about it because people from the Smithsonian Institution were at the reservation talking about our culture and exhibits for their new American Indian Museum. Their interest in preserving our culture got us talking about the loss of our language. Rita mentioned that she had been taken out of classes during elementary school and said, "Why can't the same thing be done for our kids so we can teach them our language?" The idea was later presented to the Acting Director of Seminole Education, Barb Wilmes, who said, "I don't know why we couldn't do this."

In a separate incident, high school student Andrew Bowers talked to Phoebe Raulerson, the superintendent of the Okeechobee public schools, at a science fair. He had done a study about the Creek language for his project. They got into a discussion about how the Seminoles were losing their language, and it made her aware of our need for a pullout program.

Before we made contact with Florida State Department of Education in Tallahassee, we had the blessing of Mrs. Raulerson. After making some phone calls to Tallahassee, we flew there to talk about our ideas and were encouraged to pursue our reservation classes. We would involve community members, including teachers and helpers who would get time off from their jobs to participate. We wanted this to be our program and feature our own people as language and culture teachers. We met again with the superintendent to let her know about our visit and curriculum plans. Mrs. Raulerson later wrote:

> Members of the Seminole Tribe want to develop a plan to teach their children their native language one day each week, while emphasizing the Sunshine State Standards of Florida. It would be a great loss to Florida and to the United States to lose this language. We commend the Seminole Tribe for their efforts, and as a school system, we will work with them in any way possible.

Our Seminole educators recognize that taking our students out of school one day a week is a risk. We hope that the students will gain self-esteem about who they are. We also hope that the students will find academic subjects more relevant and therefore easier to understand. We decided to use one full day a week, because that was the most time we expected the school to allow us to pull out the students. We are lucky to have that. The teachers might not be crazy about the idea, but the superintendent is very supportive of our efforts. To help the teachers we selected Friday to hold our own classes because on Friday, the students usually get wound up over field trips and special events. Having the classes on Friday would allow the kids to have the weekend to calm down before returning to their regular classes on Monday.

## THE SURVEY

Next we made a survey to determine parental interest in keeping children on the reservation on each Friday of the school year to learn language and culture. The survey was handed out on the school bus to the Okeechobee public school students to give to their parents. Parents had to return their answers to the education mailbox, offices, or bus driver. Of the surveys handed out, 40% were returned.

All of the parents who returned the survey thought we should preserve our language. All thought we should teach Seminole history. Most important, all of those responding said they would allow their children to attend the pullout program one day a week. One comment was an emphatic "Finally!" Another said it was "a very good idea." Of the twelve parents responding, half said that someone in their household spoke either Creek (seven) or Mikasuki, indicating that at least some students would receive reinforcement at home.

## COMMUNITY INVOLVEMENT

Members of the community will be teachers, using the language and talking about our natural environment, our use of numbers, our history, our government, and our values and customs. The education staff will work with the county schools to develop a curriculum around traditional knowledge using the language. Exercises will relate the traditional knowledge to science, math, reading, and writing. This system is modeled on the educational method known as the Language Experience Approach and on the integrative education method discussed by Oscar Kawagley and others regarding Yup'ik education in Alaska (Kwagley 1995; Benjamin, Pecos, and Romero 1996; Wahlberg 1997).

Like the Hawaiian language immersion schools (Hinton 2001), we hope to teach in our language. Although this is the best way to learn a second language, at first our teachers will experience as much difficulty as the students. We will have to learn to speak slowly, to praise the successes, and to ignore the mispronunciations and errors. We will encourage the whole community to use the language and provide regular opportunities to practice simple exchanges with the students.

What will be the outcome? We hope that the children will be able to read and write the language and to speak it in simple conversation. Our success will be our community's success. We hope that a byproduct of the classes will be increased self-esteem, a sense of pride in being Seminole, and increased confidence in their ability to perform in the local schools.

In addition, we will encourage the children to teach their parents. Members will help with field trips, cooking, organization, and special activities, and they will make an effort to speak the language everywhere.

Although some adults might not like the idea of writing down our language, writing is another tool for learning language. It is important because some people understand the language but can't speak it. If they learn the alphabet and learn to read and write the language, with practice they should be able to learn to speak it as well. With the development of written native language material, we can write books to reinforce learning long before students can converse with ease. Because acquisition depends on exposure, books will provide an opportunity for students who do not have language speakers in the home. Language will become more permanent with written material (Peacock and Day 1999). Languages with literary traditions survive longer (Anonby 1999). Cherokee leader and syllabary creator Sequoyah recognized the power of the written word that the white man held. The desire to write treaties in a language his people could understand inspired him to develop a written language for Cherokee.

## OUR METHODS

The program focuses on kindergarten through fifth grade. This choice is based on the view that it is easier to acquire another language before the "Critical Period" of adolescence has passed. Yule suggests that optimum years for learning occur from ages ten to sixteen, when students may still have "'flexibility' of the language acquisition faculty" (Yule 2000:192) and cognitive maturity of language skills. We believe that some students will adopt the second language with more facility because of their "passive" understanding of the meaning of Creek through contact with monolingual grandparents or other frequent Creek speakers. They are expected to be more open to learning.

Younger children are less self conscious than teenagers, who sometimes feel embarrassment at being unable to speak their native language or pronounce the words with fluency. Younger children may lack inhibition against pronouncing sounds not found in English, such as the /p/, /v/, /g/, and /r/ sounds in Creek. Earlier bilingual speakers of Creek and English may have been reluctant to retain their traditional language because of the affective filter. Experiences of teasing from mispronounced English words may have caused negative emotions, just as new Creek speakers may now feel uncomfortable, stressed, or unmotivated to learn the language. To create an atmosphere of learning, the program will involve the younger children by having them remain on the reservation for the day program and use language through cultural items with native speakers. Reading and assignment materials will be developed by fluent speakers out of stories, crafts, and daily life on the reservation.

Our communicative approach (Yule 2000:193–94) is to make language learning more interesting and less artificial. The teaching methods will rely not on a "pattern-practice" approach, conscious learning, or grammar, but on creating a communicative experience in the classroom. Students will be introduced to functions of the language, organized around concepts such as how to ask for something or how to give commands in a social context. Patterned sentences of word substitution will emphasize the language structure in interesting ways rather than rote learning. The first book written for the program in Creek, *Naken Hompet Cv* ("What do you eat?"), uses this technique.

The other method to be used is to focus on the learner and to tolerate mistakes. Making the language fun and tolerating errors are key to inviting usage. Unusual combinations of words and unusual word order may indicate that the speaker is making an active effort to communicate or form new meaning from known generalizations, yet missing the nuances of prefixes or suffixes, pluralization, and so on. Some mistakes may favor previously learned English structure. All attempts will be acknowledged with little emphasis on "correction." Communication is the objective.

Through the tolerance of errors comes success by encouraging attempts and accomplishment. Meeting success will motivate language learners to learn. Students will be encouraged to guess—to risk making errors in order to communicate. Classroom activities will center on having students interact with each other, completing tasks together.

Finally, communicative competence will be experienced using grammatical competence, sociolinguistic competence, and strategic competence. Grammatical competence will rely on using the words and structure of Creek accurately. Sociolinguistic competence will provide the social context for phrases and words; for example, a speaker will know the situation in which to ask for something or to demand it. Strategic competence refers to the ability to organize a message or redefine meaning to communicate. If a person cannot remember a specific word, a strategy that could be used would be to describe the item.

## ASSESSMENT

The curriculum will be built around state readiness standards with particular attention paid to the most appropriate topics for connecting to Seminole customs and values. Students will receive grades for their performance. Staff will develop methods of assessing progress for each level. Successful completion and retention of information will be measured at the end of each term. Cooperative study, peer mentoring, and noncompetitive activities will reflect traditional social learning. Language learning will emphasize conversation.

The curriculum will also feature many elements of culture. Possible topics include government organization and responsibility, cattle raising, traditional religion, tribal enterprises, reservation activities, natural science, geography, history, crafts, kinship, and values. Different community members have already started planning their information, developing materials, and volunteering their time.

The scope of the project we propose is ambitious, but possible. As interest in reviving our language builds, more and more members of our community are likely to become involved. Our parents, our leaders, and our school administrators support us. Now we must support our language. Our Creek language is symbolic of our culture and a means of communicating our worldview (Hickerson 2000). Our efforts will produce a source of cultural awareness and pride. To quote MariJo Moore, Cherokee poet, author, and journalist:

> If you take away a people's language, take away the way they think, then they are no longer who they really are, regardless of skin color or blood quantum. . . . Our language did not diminish overnight. [Restoring the language] will take time, dedication, and lots of work. (1999:19)

## ADDENDUM

Since this paper was initially written, the plan has been implemented and two days of teaching completed. The program has tentatively been given a Creek name, *Pemahyetv,* which means "Our Way." Late summer meetings with the principal and teachers stressed the need to link language and culture work to Florida readiness standards or Florida Comprehensive Assessment Tests guidelines. Parents and Seminole teachers are nervous that the children's grades might decrease if they are not in public school one day a week. The schools have great confidence in the program and simply ask us to stress that the students and parents be conscientious about public school attendance the other four days. Public school teachers will provide makeup sessions on Monday to accommodate the program.

Pullout teachers create lesson plans two weeks ahead of time. They know intuitively what to teach about language and culture but have more difficulty integrating the written state standards, which are listed in the abstract and not specific enough to be easily understood. The thick volume of the standards is intimidating in itself. Themes for the first two months are Seminole values and the Seminoles' place in the world. After observing the efforts throughout the day and seeing the children's enthusiasm, we perceive the program as positive.

Since the classes of September 6 and September 13, 2002, have been completed, some assessment can be made. The sense of pride among the teachers echoes through their post-teaching meetings, although they are tired at the end of the day and have many more questions for the group. Most problems concern logistics rather than teaching language or culture. Issues that dominate the conversations include lunch monitoring procedures, integration of students who need special education help, grading methods, student storage space for daily work, arranging for enough seating, and organizing after-school dropoff. Specific students are praised for their ability to learn the language quickly. Some are found to pronounce well or have more than a rudimentary knowledge of Creek.

Teachers remark that it is difficult to provide enough short activities to fill the class time for kindergarten students. When the end of their attention span arrives, some teachers take them for slow walks to their next class. This is a viable solution to restlessness for all the classes, because several students query, "When do we get recess?" Recess was not planned into the day, but the teachers are encouraged to use it as they deem necessary to diffuse excess energy.

Already the Seminole leaders have visited the school to encourage the students. Each has regret about not speaking their language or not knowing it well enough. Immersion is not complete, yet many instructions, stories, and songs are used daily. The goal is immersion, but the teachers are delaying full immersion until students have mastered simple instructions.

The program's worth is confirmed when we observe students sitting in rapt attention listening to a Seminole elder telling them in both Creek and English about the traditional medicine. They are remembering it as "Seminole Science." It is "Our Way."

## REFERENCES

Anonby, Stan J. 1999. Reversing Language Shift: Can Kwak'wala Be Revived? In *Revitalizing Indigenous Languages,* ed. Jon Reyhner, Gina Cantoni, Robert N. St. Clair, and Evangeline Parsons Yazzie, pp. 33–52. Flagstaff: Northern Arizona University.

Benjamin, Rebecca, Regis Pecos, and Mary Eunice Romero. 1996. Language Revitalization Efforts in the Pueblo de Cochiti: Becoming "Literate" in an Oral Society. In *Indigenous Literacies in the Americas: Language Planning from the Bottom Up,* ed. N. Hornberger, pp. 114–36. New York: Mouton.

Hickerson, Nancy. 2000. *Linguistic Anthropology.* 2nd ed. Fort Worth, Texas: Harcourt College Publishers.

Hinton, Leanne. 2001. Hawaiian Language Schools. In *Native American Voices: A Reader,* ed. S. Lobo and S. Talbot, pp. 520–31. Upper Saddle River, N.J.: Prentice Hall.

Kawagley, A. Oscar. 1995. *A Yupiaq Worldview: Pathway to Ecology and Spirit.* Prospect Heights, Ill.: Waveland.

Moore, MariJo. 1999. Preschool Program Revitalizing Cherokee Language. *Cultural Survival Quarterly* 23(3):19.

Nettle, Daniel, and Suzanne Romaine. 2000. *Vanishing Voices: The Extinction of the World's Languages*. New York: Oxford University Press.

Peacock, Thomas D., and Donald R. Day. 1999. Teaching American Indian and Alaska Native Languages in the Schools: What Has Been Learned. ERIC digest, EDO RC 99-10, December. http://www.ael.org/eric/digests/endorc9910.htm, accessed 30 September 2003.

Shorris, Earl. 2000. The Last Word: Can the World's Small Languages Be Saved? *Harper's Magazine,* August, 35–43.

Stans, Susan E. 1996. *The Cultures of Drinking within a Native American Community.* Ph.D. dissertation, University of Florida, Gainesville.

Wahlberg, Natasia. 1997. Teaching and Preserving Yup'ik traditional Literacy. In *Indigenous Literacies in the Americas: Language Planning from the Bottom Up,* ed. N. Hornberger. Berlin: Mouton de Gruyter.

Yule, George. 2000. *The Study of Language*. Cambridge: Cambridge University Press.

# Medicine-Making Language among the Muskogee: The Effects of Changing Attitudes

*Pamela Innes*

Linguists and members of Native American communities are well aware that many indigenous languages are endangered (Lanoue 1991; Hale et al. 1992; Pye 1992; Hinton 1998; McCarty and Zepeda 1999). Native communities have reacted to the threat of language loss in a number of different ways, the majority of which create or recognize discourse genres in which the native language is the primary code. The Yuchi, as Jackson and Linn have noted, continue to use Yuchi in the "calls" that broadcast announcements to stompground members. In general, however, Yuchi people use English as their code for the majority of ritual and nonritual discourse (Jackson and Linn 2000:63–65). Kroskrity (1993) has found that the Tewa utilize Spanish and English as their primary codes but retain Tewa for ritual interaction. Hill and Hill (1986) have found that Nahuatl is retained by indigenous people in Central Mexico for interaction with family and close acquaintances, while Spanish is the dominant language for interaction with people from outside the local community and for commercial interaction. By delineating discourse genres in which the native language *must* be used, these and many other communities promote use of the language in limited situations and demonstrate social support for the language's continued use. (For the importance of maintaining venues for language use in retaining endangered languages, see Fishman 1972 and Dorian 1989.)

The Muskogee find themselves in a situation similar to that found among the indigenous people of Central Mexico and the Tewa. There are still approximately three thousand speakers of Mvskoke, and some children are still learning Mvskoke as their first language (Martin 2002).[1] However, the Muskogee recognize that their language is threatened, and the majority of the people with whom I work admit some unease about the future of their language. Older members of the community note that fewer and fewer children are learning the language and that the number of fully fluent middle-aged speakers also is in decline. For members of the stompdance community, the loss of the language is most salient when applied to medicine making, as this activity is central to the continuation of the stompdance community itself.

The members of the Muskogee stompdance community are a subset of the general Muskogee community. Stompdance members are distinguished from other members of the community by their attendance at religious ceremonies performed at stompgrounds located within the area bounded by the Muskogee (Creek) Nation. Three Christian sects have become well established within the Muskogee community as well: the Baptists, the Methodists, and the Presbyterians. Stompdancers are distinct from members of these Christian sects in that their religious rituals consist of four night-long dances held at each ground during the summer months, at which medicine is taken to promote or maintain the health of all members of the stompground hosting the dances. Membership at a stompground does not necessarily keep one from participating in church activities, and vice versa. Many stompground members attend Muskogee and/or Seminole churches during the winter months and when their ground is not sponsoring a dance, and church members are seen at dances throughout the season.

From the beginning of my work in the stompdance community in 1992, people would comment that there may not be medicine men for much longer, precisely because younger men were not learning the formulaic chants and songs appropriate for particular kinds of medicines. The concern about the decreasing numbers of fluent Mvskoke speakers is associated with this concern about a decrease in the numbers of medicine men because of a generally held belief that one must be fluent in Mvskoke before beginning to learn the medicine-making language. As work on ideologies of other linguistic communities (Woolard and Schieffelin 1994; Mühlhäusler 1998; Schieffelin, Woolard, and Kroskrity 1998; Hill 1999; Kroskrity 2000) would lead us to expect, the ideology asserting the necessity of Mvskoke fluency for apprentices serves to maintain and reinforce the position of Mvskoke as an important marker of Muskogee identity. It also places a restriction on the population who would be eligible to achieve the status of medicine man, which reinforces Muskogee ideas about "traditional" Muskogee values and practices. Because some stompdance community members are communicating a different attitude, however, I have come to wonder whether this different attitude will lead to fewer or greater numbers of men learning medicine-making language and what kinds of effects this may have on conceptualizations of what constitutes a "true" Muskogee identity.

A decreased insistence that a medicine man's apprentice must first be fluent also may signal a general shift in attitude regarding the preservation of Mvskoke. One can ask whether the change in ideology regarding Mvskoke fluency and apprenticing with a medicine man is a sign of resignation about the future loss of Mvskoke, an adapting mechanism adopted because of the lower number of fluent speakers, or a little of both. Some tentative answers to these questions and outcomes resulting from the answers are explored below.

## THE MUSKOGEE COMMUNITY

The Muskogee formerly inhabited the Southeastern states of Georgia, Alabama, and Florida. Along with the other Southeastern tribes, they were removed to Oklahoma (Indian Territory) in the early nineteenth century. The Muskogee were provided land in the eastern part of Oklahoma. As a result of several treaties, the current land base of the Muskogee (Creek) Nation is located within eight counties in eastern Oklahoma: Hughes, McIntosh, Muskogee, Okmulgee, Okfuskee, Creek, Tulsa, and Wagoner.

Shortly after Removal, the Muskogee reestablished their traditional social units: the tribal towns. Each town, *tvlwv* in Mvskoke, was the locus of political and economic decision making, religious ritual, and kinship structures. Membership in a town was matrilineal, and one was surrounded by clan relatives when in one's own town. Until the establishment of the General Council in 1867, individual towns were free to determine their own political and economic activities, an arrangement that continued the structure found before Removal. Also, located within or close to each town was its dance ground, where the religious rituals were held. Membership in a town granted membership at a particular dance ground.

Allotment, the outcome of the Dawes Act, divided the towns in the late nineteenth and early twentieth centuries. Individual families had to choose tracts of land from which they would make their living. Many townspeople had to choose tracts quite distant from other townspeople, simply because of the geography of the area and the need for productive agricultural land. The dispersal of town members caused many towns to become dispersed as well, with only the stompground (dance ground) providing a locus of social interaction for all town members during the summer dances. It is not unusual for current members of a stompground to relate that their ground is all that remains of the geographical features of town membership. Muskogee and Seminole churches also were affiliated with particular towns, and church members are able to relate stories about church membership being tied to town affiliation (Schultz 1999).

## THE MEDICINE MAN'S ROLE AT THE GROUND

When a dance is taking place, the medicine man working for the ground hosting the dance will have made medicines to be used by ground members before and after the dance. The content of these medicines varies somewhat from ground to ground, and each ground has some form of medicine. Only dances during the wintertime (social dances) are held without use of these medicines. The medicines maintain the health and well-being of all ground members who use them, and the efficacy of a ground's medicine is supposed to be observable through the correct conduct, good health, and good lives of the ground members. If a significant number of a particular ground's members begin to have health difficulties, social problems, family problems, or psychological problems, the medicine man's abilities are often called into question by nonmembers.

The stompgrounds at which the medicine men practice their craft are generally located in rural areas. At the center of each ground is a circular area containing the central fireplace, the dance ring, and the men's arbors. Medicines, placed underneath the fireplace during the establishment of the ground at that particular spot, protect the ground and guard those who dance there from harm. These medicines can be removed from their spot under the fireplace and moved to a new location only by a medicine man who knows the correct chants, actions, and songs appropriate for that particular ground's medicine. This central area is ritually cleaned and treated with medicine at certain points in the ceremonial season, a practice that reflects the religious character of the stompground. Around this central area are arranged the camps and seating areas for guests at the dances. This area, with all items located in it, is considered to be less sacred, though there are rules for conduct that apply to people located in this area.

Language plays a very important role in the making of medicine. Among Southeastern peoples, medicine is made by decocting plants and plant products in water (Mooney 1890; Speck 1911:212–14; Mooney and Olbrechts 1932; Howard and Lena 1984). In order to energize these decoctions and cause them to become efficacious medicines, a medicine man must blow into the liquid and chant or sing over it (Mooney 1891; Speck 1911: 211–35; Howard and Lena 1984). The medicine man's song/chant must be appropriate for the particular kind of cure wished for and for the particular plant materials used to make the decoction. Medicines for use by ground members during a dance involve linguistic practices similar to this category of medicine, including use of specific chants for a particular ground's medicine. Several medicine men have told me that each ground's medicine is somewhat different from any other's, and medicine men must know the correct chants for the ground(s) they doctor.

Some emulsions are thought to be productive without applying the linguistic feature, but these are primarily for minor irritations or common applications. For instance, sassafras tea may be taken for stomach trouble or circulation difficulties, and tea from willow bark is taken for relief of headache or fever. Women and tribal members who have not apprenticed as medicine men are aware of these remedies and state that they can be used without accompanying linguistic production. For more difficult or troublesome diseases, or for diseases thought to result from supernatural sources, a medicine man who knows the appropriate medicine for the malady, and the appropriate medicine song, will be sought to produce the cure.

## HOW MEDICINE MEN ARE TRAINED

Traditionally, men wishing to become medicine men underwent an apprenticeship lasting from a few months to a number of years (Speck 1911:212; Swanton 1928:617–18). Men approached medicine men from whom they wished to learn the botanical and verbal medicines necessary to cure maladies and offered some form of payment for the privilege of learning these medicines. The apprentices, who fasted during the time it took to learn the medicines, were taken to a remote area that precluded contact with other town members. There, they were taught the verbal formulas and botanical contents of the doctor's medicine. According to Swanton (1928:617–18), the medicine man would provide the apprentices with the verbal formulas over a period of time. The teacher would perform a portion of the medical formula for the apprentice, who then practiced reciting this portion until the medicine man's return. When the medicine man returned, he would ask the apprentice to repeat what he had learned, correcting him whenever he made mistakes. Swanton (1928:617) notes that the medicine man "did not stop [the recitations] because his pupil had repeated it correctly once but made him go over it often later, because unless it was gone over in just such a manner it would not be effective when used."

The five present-day medicine men I interviewed about work at the grounds stated that their apprenticeships lasted for at least four years so that they could remember all of the ground medicine appropriately. In each case, they approached the medicine man for a particular ground, generally the ground at which they were already members, and offered him some payment for his knowledge. Each was required to fast and to remain distant from other people during the period of his training, lest he be distracted from learning the medicines. During the apprenticeship, each was required to correctly perform the medicinal chants and songs several times before the medicine man considered him to have mastered the formula for any particular medicine.

JP found this practice to be irritating at first, but he came to realize how important it was as the formulas became longer and more complex. Because it is inappropriate for women still within their reproductive years to learn medicine songs and chants, I did not ask any of the medicine men to share any formulas with me. However, JP, AA, and TH all have said that there are a number of levels of difficulty in learning the songs and chants. TH and AA noted that many of the words in the medicine songs are very, very old and are not easily translatable, even by fluent Mvskoke speakers.

Two of the medicine men, TH and JP, have suggested that the use of Mvskoke words that are marked, or that differ significantly from their commonly used forms, in the medicines is part of their power. Because it is culturally inappropriate for me to ask about specific songs, I do not have any data from TH or JP regarding the use of uncommon forms of Mvskoke words in song texts that they perform. However, marked forms of Mvskoke words are evident in song texts collected by other researchers (Speck 1911; Swanton 1928). In the song for dog disease collected by William Tuggle in the late nineteenth century (cited in Swanton 1928:641–42), presented in table 1, several words appear in a marked form. The second and third syllables of the first word have been switched in position from their order in the expected form of this word—if indeed this word is 'be easy' as translated by Swanton. Also, the words for 'sickness, feeble,' 'dead,' and the final forms of 'holding him, cramping' have vowel sounds in their second syllables that differ from the expected pronunciation. It is possible that the phonological

Table 1 Song for dog disease, collected by William Tuggle

| Song, as presented in Swanton | Translation | Expected word form, as given by Swanton, using Tuggle's orthography |
|---|---|---|
| Yoh-ho-lee | Be easy | Yoleehee |
| Yoh-ho-lee | Be easy | Yoleehee |
| Yoh-ho-lee | Be easy | Yoleehee |
| Efa | Dog | Efa |
| Polsa | Sickness, feeble | Polsee |
| Thlohko | Big, large | Thlohko |
| Elahtee | Dead | Eleta |
| Hahlahtee | Cramping, holding | Hahlahtee |
| St Chay | [an interjection indicating the end of a sentence] | St Chay |
| Hoh-loh-tee | Holding him, cramping | Hahlahtee |
| Hoh-loh-tee | Holding him, cramping | Hahlahtee |
| Hoh-loh-tee | Holding him, cramping | Hahlahtee |
| St Chay | [interjection] | St Chay |

forms of these words were changed for use in the medicinal formula, so the form presented in Swanton does not simply reflect a mispronunciation or misinterpretation of the vowel sounds.

TH, AA, and JP have told me that the inclusion of marked forms of common Mvskoke words in songs cause them to devote a great deal of thought and perseverance into learning the formulas, which helps make the medicine more potent. The concentration required to use the marked forms at the appropriate points in the songs focuses a great deal of energy into the medicine as the medicine man sings over it. JP and AA are not certain that apprentices not fluent in Mvskoke will appreciate the use of marked forms because they do not know the unmarked (usual) forms, nor do they think medicine men who are not fluent in Mvskoke will work so hard to keep from using the unmarked forms as they produce a medicinal song containing marked forms. According to AA, "Thinking about the words, it makes you put good medicine in because you're thinking hard for that person and making him better."

TH stated that he had a notebook in which all of his formulas were written, a common practice among Southeastern medicine men (Mooney 1891). He stated that there were times he had to refer to his notebook in order to refresh his memory before reciting the correct formula for a particular medicine, especially those utilizing marked linguistic forms. However, his notebook was not always a foolproof solution to remembering to include marked forms; he stated that he occasionally had trouble figuring out how to write down the marked form of the word, or he forgot to write the word in the marked form altogether.

## LANGUAGE AND THE AVAILABILITY OF MEDICINE MEN

When I began working with members of the stompdance community, a common reply to my questions about concern over decreasing use of Mvskoke and/or decreasing numbers of Mvskoke speakers had to do with the problem of finding enough medicine men to officiate at the grounds. From 1992 to 1997, an overwhelming majority of members of the stompdance community, including five medicine men I frequently consulted about ceremonial practices, were adamant that young men learning to be medicine men must be fluent in Mvskoke before they began their apprenticeship. Community members assumed that the apprentice could not learn the correct form of each song or chant unless he was already fluent in Mvskoke. They also believed that the apprentices would not understand how the songs/chants caused the medicine to become efficacious unless they understood the language of the song, even when it contained archaic or marked forms of Mvskoke words.

Because apprenticing to become a medicine man is not an easy task for economic and social reasons, stompground members were concerned that few of the available young men would be willing to apprentice themselves to a practicing medicine man. The requirement of fluency in Mvskoke decreased the size of the available pool of apprentices even further. Eventually, it would seem, there would be very few or no young men willing and able to take on the task of becoming a medicine man's apprentice. Given that, there would be no new medicine men to take over as the current medicine men aged. Eventually, the stompdance community itself would become extinct because without medicine men there can be no dances.

Beginning in 1998, it came to my attention that some stompground members had begun to entertain the thought that a young man might not need to be fluent in Mvskoke before taking on the role of apprentice. Instead, some began to suggest that the apprentice could get by simply by learning the chants and songs by rote. As long as they pronounced the words correctly and in the correct order, the medicine should be just fine. Thus, the medicine songs/chants could be learned by the Berlitz method—memorize the appropriate formula for each medicine learned.

As discussed above, even men fluent in Mvskoke are required to spend a great deal of effort to memorize the words of the songs they learn in order to become medicine men. However, as TH, JP, and AA noted, the marked word forms in the songs stand out to fluent speakers of Mvskoke and cause fluent speakers to devote special care to remembering when marked forms occur in the songs. In the dog disease song, for instance, the unmarked (usual) form of 'hahlahtee' occurs at the first use of this word, but a marked form 'hohlohtee' is used three times thereafter. The fluent speaker must recognize that the unmarked form of the word does appear in the song, remember that it is the first use of this word, and that marked forms of the word are used subsequently. I would argue that fluent speakers of Mvskoke are struck by the alternation of marked and unmarked forms in these songs, which makes them more conscious of the sacred nature of these songs than those not fluent in Mvskoke would be.

In 1999, I began to ask specifically about whether men not fluent in Mvskoke were being trained as medicine men at any of the grounds. Each of the three surviving medicine men out of the five I originally worked with and twenty-one of thirty-eight general members of stompgrounds have told me of grounds at which they believe this practice is taking place. When this was mentioned, I asked individuals what they thought about the efficacy and safety of medicine made by the nonfluent apprentices. This is an important question because of the effect medicine has on all ground members and on those who seek individual treatment for diseases and other maladies. One would suspect that those who strongly believe that only those already fluent in Mvskoke can learn the verbal formulas requisite for a powerful, curative medication will believe that the apprentices' medicines will be ineffective and possibly dangerous. On the other hand, those who do not believe that an apprentice must be fully fluent in Mvskoke will assume the apprentices' medicines are efficacious and safe.

Thirteen of the twenty-one ground members who told me about grounds at which nonfluent men are learning to make medicine, and each of the three medicine men, stated that the apprentice must be fluent in Mvskoke. Ten of these thirteen ground members and two of the three medicine men said that they would not attend dances at the grounds identified as having nonfluent apprentices. Uncertainty about the safety of the medicine being taken at these grounds was cited by all of these individuals as a reason for not attending dances at these grounds. Three ground members and one of the medicine men mentioned that they were worried about the decision-making abilities of the medicine men at these grounds because they were teaching medicine-making language to men not fluent in Mvskoke. Five ground members said that they were worried about the grounds' leaders' willingness to make such a drastic break with tradition.

Eleven of the ground members and one of the medicine men admitted to attending dances at some of the grounds they have identified as having nonfluent apprentices. The members and medicine man stated that because no misfortunes or severe illnesses had struck members of these grounds, they believed the medicine at these grounds to be safe. Two of the ground members expressed some uncertainty about the future safety of the medicine at these grounds when the apprentices become the medicine men and are solely responsible for making the medicine. However, these same members stated that they would feel comfortable continuing to attend dances at these grounds if nothing untoward happened to their friends who are members of these grounds.

Only three of the thirteen ground members and one of the three medicine men who stated that they believed apprentices must be fluent in Mvskoke admitted to attending dances at grounds they thought were training nonfluent apprentices. Those ground members who had *not* stated the same belief all acknowledged attending grounds they thought were training nonfluent apprentices. Some of these individuals may have held but not voiced such a belief. However, because I had asked these individuals specifically about such a belief, it is reasonable to assume that they do not hold it.

Interestingly, I interviewed six individuals who are members of two grounds identified by others as having nonfluent apprentices. None of these individuals thought that a man not fluent in Mvskoke was apprenticing with their medicine man, and each identified other grounds as places where this was happening. Each of these six thought it was a shortcoming at a ground to have to resort to training men not fluent in Mvskoke, but no one immediately called the safety of the ground members into question. At the time, each of the six thought that their own ground's leaders and medicine man were concerned about training new men, but each also noted that their medicine man was in good health and was not in immediate need of replacement. Each of the six also identified two or more male ground members fluent in Mvskoke who might be willing to become apprentices when training a new medicine man became a greater concern.

## RAMIFICATIONS FOR LANGUAGE RETENTION

Within the past four years, there has been a shift in the stompground members' opinions about the need for an apprentice to exhibit fluency in Mvskoke prior to beginning his training as a medicine man. The above data show that just over half of the sample (twenty-four of forty-one people, including both ground members and medicine men) thought that local ideology was changing and that men were being trained in medicine-making songs and chants without having prior fluency in Mvskoke. Those who think that apprentice medicine men need not be fluent in Mvskoke do not profess any worries about the safety of the medicine produced by these men once they have completed their training, nor do they worry about attending dances at grounds they think have nonfluent apprentices.

This change in opinion about the necessity of fluency for apprentices may signal a general change in opinion about the need to retain Mvskoke as the primary code in other genres. Many of the stompground members I interviewed expressed some feeling of inadequacy regarding their use of English. One man, HH, told me that he wants his children to speak and read English better than he does because he believes his English-language skills have held him back economically. He says that he wants his children to be able to understand Mvskoke because they should be able to understand what their elders are telling them, but he does not express a belief that the ability to speak the language will further their education or their careers.

I heard similar comments from elders and middle-aged ground members about their own parents' views on the English language, yet many of these same individuals grew up in households in which Mvskoke was still spoken and children were still expected to use Mvskoke. However, conversations in Mvskoke are being conducted less frequently at the stompgrounds, in community meetings, and at Muskogee churches. It would appear that the Muskogee discourses about the importance of English for advancement (Silverstein 1998:136) are being realized in social practice, rather than simply presented as an ideological stance or imagistic canon. That Muskogee people are using English in situations and genres where Mvskoke was once the language of choice suggests that people have internalized the view that English allows for greater advancement to such an extent that its use in arenas where Mvskoke was once necessary for advancement is no longer questioned. Indeed, it would appear that the ideological power of English, which had been voiced but not so openly pursued in earlier times, is now being actively played out in the real world of the Muskogee community.

This change is alarming from a language-retention point of view because Muskogee accommodation of this variation in the realm of their traditional grounds signals a willingness to give up the primacy of Mvskoke in what many ground members have described as an important linguistic venue. As explained by a member at one of the Muskogee grounds,

> The grounds, that's where the real life goes on. We're the ones who keep this culture going, and we're how come the Muskogee are still here. These practices, this making medicine and dancing to pray, that's what makes us Muskogee and what keeps the world going. Those leaders, the medicine men, the mēkkos [ground chiefs], the hennehvs [assistant leaders], they all have to be traditional and speak their language. That's a problem with these younger ones, they don't know how to talk, and it keeps them from learning how to lead out here. (FG, interview, 22 June 1996)

Until 1998, this assertion that the use of Mvskoke was vital to the continued strength and existence of the stompgrounds and that the grounds were equated with continued existence of the Muskogee community was voiced by all of the members I asked about these points. In their eyes, loss of the Mvskoke language would lead to death of the grounds, and the Muskogee community would no longer exist.[2]

Now, however, with the seeming shift in ideology about apprentice fluency, the language is being allowed to wane without threatening the existence of the grounds or, perhaps, the larger Muskogee community. While one can accept that this is a nice way to allow for continuation of the grounds despite the fact that there are fewer Mvskoke speakers, it also appears to allow for a lessening of concern about the loss of the language. The shift may, indeed, indicate that the Muskogee are becoming somewhat complacent about language endangerment.

## NOTES

1. References to the language are written as the term appears in the writing system preferred by literate Muskogee so as to differentiate the language, Mvskoke, from the tribal identity.

2. Note, however, that in FG's own discussion of the importance of carrying on the language, he uses the English plural morpheme /-s/ on the Mvskoke words for ground leaders, rather than using the Mvskoke plural morpheme /-vlke ~ -vke/. This was probably done for my benefit as an English speaker; I have heard FG produce many examples of morphologically correct Mvskoke plurals.

## REFERENCES

Dorian, Nancy C., ed. 1989. *Investigating Obsolescence: Studies in Language Contraction and Death.* Cambridge: Cambridge University Press.

Fishman, Joshua A. 1972. *Language in Sociocultural Change.* Sel. and introd. by A. S. Dil. Stanford, Calif.: Stanford University Press.

Foster, Michael K. 1989. When Words Become Deeds: An Analysis of Three Iroquois Longhouse Speech Events. In *Explorations in the Ethnography of Speaking,* 2nd ed., ed. R. Bauman and J. Sherzer. Cambridge: Cambridge University Press.

Hale, Ken, Michael Krauss, Lucille Watahomigie, Akira Yamamoto, Colette Craig, La Verne Masayesva Jeanne, and Nora C. England. 1992. Endangered Languages. *Language* 68(1):1–42.

Hill, Jane H., and Kenneth C. Hill. 1986. *Speaking Mexicano: Dynamics of Syncretic Language in Central Mexico.* Tucson: University of Arizona Press.

Hill, Jane H. 1999. Styling Locally, Styling Globally: What Does It Mean? *Journal of Sociolinguistics* 3(4):542–57.

Hinton, Leanne. 1998. Part 1. Indigenous Languages in the USA—Language Loss and Revitalization in California: Overview. *International Journal of the Sociology of Language* 132:83–95.

Howard, James H., and Willie Lena. 1984. *Oklahoma Seminoles: Medicines, Magic, and Religion.* Norman: University of Oklahoma Press.

Jackson, Jason B., and Mary S. Linn. 2000. Calling in the Members: Linguistic Form and Cultural Context in a Yuchi Ritual Speech Genre. *Anthropological Linguistics* 42(1):61–80.

Kroskrity, Paul V. 1993. *Language, History, and Identity: Ethnolinguistic Studies of the Arizona Tewa.* Tucson: University of Arizona Press.

———. 1998. Arizona Tewa Kiva Speech as a Manifestation of a Dominant Language Ideology. In *Language Ideologies: Practice and Theory,* ed. B. B. Schieffelin, K. A. Woolard, and P. V. Kroskrity, pp. 103–22. Oxford: Oxford University Press.

———. 2000. *Regimes of Language: Ideologies, Polities, and Identities.* Santa Fe: School of American Research Press.

Lanoue, G. 1991. Language Loss, Language Gain: Cultural Camouflage and Social Change among the Sekani of Northern British Columbia. *Language in Society* 20(1):87–116.

Martin, Jack B. 2002. Creek Ways of Speaking. Paper presented at Southern Anthropological Society Meetings. Asheville, North Carolina.

McCarty, Teresa L., and Ofelia Zepeda. 1999. Amerindians. In *Handbook of Language and Ethnic Identity,* ed. J. Fishman, pp. 197–210. Oxford: Oxford University Press.

Mooney, James. 1890. *Cherokee Theory and Practice of Medicine*. Cambridge: Riverside.

———. 1891. *The Sacred Formulas of the Cherokee*. Bureau of Ethnology 7th Annual Report. Washington, D.C.: Government Printing Office.

Mooney, James, and Frans M. Olbrechts. 1932. *The Swimmer Manuscript: Cherokee Sacred Formulas and Medicinal Prescriptions*. Bureau of American Ethnology, Bulletin 99. Washington, D.C.: Government Printing Office.

Mühlhäusler, Peter. 1998. Layer upon Layer of Languages. *Journal of Pidgin and Creole Languages* 13:1–8.

Opler, Morris E. 1952. The Creek "Town" and the Problem of Creek Indian Political Reorganization. In *Human Problems in Technological Change,* ed. E. H. Spicer, pp. 165–80. New York: Russell Sage Foundation.

———. 1987. Report on the History and Contemporary State of Aspects of Creek Social Organization and Government. [1937]. Reprinted in *A Creek Source Book,* ed. W. C. Sturtevant, pp. 30–75. New York: Garland.

Pye, Clifton. 1992. Language Loss among the Chilcotin. *International Journal of the Sociology of Language* 93:75–86.

Schieffelin, Bambi B., Kathryn A. Woolard, and Paul V. Kroskrity, eds. 1998. *Language Ideologies: Practice and Theory.* Oxford: Oxford University Press.

Schultz, Jack M. 1999 *The Seminole Baptist Churches of Oklahoma: Maintaining a Traditional Community.* Norman: University of Oklahoma Press.

Silverstein, Michael. 1998. The Uses and Utility of Ideology: A Commentary. In *Language Ideologies: Practice and Theory,* ed. B. B. Schieffelin, K. A. Woolard, and P. V. Kroskrity, pp. 123–45. Oxford: Oxford University Press.

Speck, Frank G. 1911. *Ceremonial Songs of the Creek and Yuchi Indians*. University of Pennsylvania Museum Anthropological Publications, vol. 1, no. 2. Philadelphia: Pennsylvania University Museum.

Swanton, John R. 1928. *Religious Beliefs and Medical Practices of the Creek Indians*. 42nd Annual Report of the Bureau of American Ethnology. Washington, D.C.: Government Printing Office.

Woolard, Kathryn A., and Bambi B. Schieffelin. 1994. Language Ideology. *Annual Review of Anthropology* 23(1):55–83.

# Not with a Southern Accent: Cajun English and Ethnic Identity

*Shana Walton*

This chapter examines dialect shifting, exaggeration, and performance in a storytelling round among friends and neighbors gathered around the coffee pot in a local convenience store early one morning in a small south Louisiana hamlet down Bayou Terrebonne. The storytelling round is a window on how *Cajun,* as an emergent ethnic identity, is negotiated, exchanged, and enacted in a speech community. The idea of *Cajun* or *Cajunness* is not just a term of local value, but has become a fixed national identity, understood like people "know" a Brooklyn accent, Italian food, or Irish music. *Cajun* is a commodity somehow "owned" and circulated by consumers of American popular culture, and, as Americans, by Acadians themselves (see Puckett in this volume for a discussion of language as commodity).

And yet the Acadians talking in this story round are also full participants in middle-class white American culture and have what some sociologists call "optional ethnicity" (Alba 1990; Waters 1990). Among other identities, they layer on "Cajun," "white," "Southern," and "American."[1]

> Non-Cajun visitors to south Louisiana often must reassess their expectations in the light of certain realities. . . . They are surprised at the Cajuns' love of fried chicken and iced tea, forgetting that this is the American South; at their love of hamburgers and Coke, forgetting that this is the United States. . . . The most consistent element in Cajun country may well be an uncanny ability to swim in the mainstream. (Ancelet, Edwards, and Pitre 1991:xvii–xviii)

In a context of crumbling economic and lifestyle differences between Acadian and "American" lifestyles, language shift and exaggeration provide subtle ways to assert an ethnicity of difference. This analysis looks at how one group of Acadians use language shifts to project an image of themselves in relation to whatever image of ethnicity is being conversationally created. This projection is against a backdrop of well-known and internalized stereotypes, circulated commodities packaged in linguistic markers. These shifts work for insiders and cultural outsiders. The shifts in and of themselves convey a meaning of difference, even to people who are not particularly familiar with that regional/ethnic speech style and cannot judge whether a shift is "right" or "wrong." I believe that ethnographic and other research data show an alignment between ethnic pride and the use of Cajun English. However, this alignment between a dialect and identity is not straightforward. Through a careful examination of the layered positionings in these stories, I hope to show some of the complexities of asserting and negotiating an ethnic identity.

## BACKGROUND

Hundreds of Acadian, or Cajun, people settled in south Louisiana in the 1700s after being driven from their homes in Nova Scotia.[2] Without a doubt one of the most distinguishing features of this cultural group has been the retention of the mother tongue, Cajun French, after more than two hundred years of living in an English-dominated world. The percentages of Acadians speaking French began to decline in the twentieth century, first with English-only enforcement in public schools, and then even more rapidly after World War II. Currently only a very few elderly Acadians are monolingual in Cajun French, and few children are fluent bilinguals. The Acadian people have been undergoing an ethnic revitalization movement since the 1970s, focused particularly on the revitalization of the French language but also on the preservation and promotion of traditional music and foodways. In fact, "Cajuns" were legally declared an ethnic group by U.S. District Judge Edwin Hunter in a July 1980 decision, *Dresser v. Roach Industries*.

In addition, activists rehabilitated the image of the Cajun nationally to such an extent that Acadians have attained some national chic. The "cool Cajun" label has coalesced locally and nationally into a stereotype of people who are French-speaking, folksy, down-to-earth, a bit exotic, and fun-loving with a propensity for being "hot-blooded" or downright violent. These characteristics are viewed as both positive and negative but are seldom or never associated with education, power, or sophistication.

During the 1980s, under the leadership of James Domengeaux, the Council for the Development of French in Louisiana (CODOFIL) became one of the leading voices promoting Louisiana's French heritage. Domengeaux believed that preserving the language was key to preserving the culture (Dorman 1984). In its early years, CODOFIL taught international French. Today CODOFIL supports the Acadian French language and culture movement. Louisiana State University, the state's flagship university, has recently instituted a Cajun studies program, directed by Acadian activist Amanda LaFleur, and is now offering Acadian French among its language courses. Arguably the revitalization movement has been, at least in part, a success. There have been increases in percentages of people willing to self-identify as "Cajun" (Trépanier 1991), in the number of outlets for traditional Acadian music, in the importance placed on French, and in the number of youths who are speaking French (Henry and Bankston 1999).[3] Louisiana's Acadians have worked hard to preserve and perpetuate Cajun French, and French is without a doubt the symbolic language of Louisiana's Acadians.

Despite the revitalization movement and popular prestige, the strongest continuing push within Acadian society over the last fifty years has been movement toward status as mainstream, middle-class Americans. As with many ethnic groups, there is a push-pull effect to a traditional identity. In the case of Cajuns, this ambivalence is exacerbated by the high profile of Cajun culture, increases in tourism, and opposition between the economic and prestige rewards of being Cajun and the very different but equally real economic and social rewards of being unhyphenated "white" American. Louisiana's Acadians will never return to the French-dominant communities of the years before the 1960s. Acadians live their public lives—work, school, church—in English.

## CAJUN ENGLISH

Cajun English is an ethnic contact dialect (Pennfield and Ornstein-Galicia 1985) that carries ethnic identity meanings. At one time, the phonological and syntactical variations from standard English could have been attributed to the underlying stratum of French. But now, like Chicano English and other dialects, Cajun English is a language variety that is itself passed down in the community. And as language varieties do, this variety and its particular markers have taken on social meaning (see Hazen in this volume for a discussion of similar processes at work in Appalachian English). As Dubois and Horvath (1999:306) note, "If identity is to be signaled by language, then it is left to English to accomplish this task because most younger speakers interact with outsiders as well as their friends and immediate family members in English." At one point during the revitalization movement, legislator Sonny "La La" Lalonde introduced a bill to declare Cajuns a legal minority in the state. A reporter asked how someone would know if he was a Cajun or not. Representative Lalonde said, "Just listen to me talk." Through fieldwork, researchers have noted particular linguistic features that mark Cajun English (Scott 1992; Walton 1994; Dubois and Horvath 1998, 1999). These features include the following:

interdental fricatives become dental stops ("dis," "dat," and "ting")

lack of aspiration on stops

nasalization

flat intonation on stressed syllables

phrase-final stress

As noted earlier, Louisiana's Acadians are located in the midst of another stigmatized language variety, Southern English, and have many of those linguistic markers as well.

## CAJUN ENGLISH AND ETHNIC IDENTITY

Self-ascription as a Cajun is often defined by ancestry, blood lines, cultural affiliation, or language. French is the symbolic language and was at one time a defining characteristic of being Acadian, but today we cannot quickly dismiss Lalonde's casual statement that referenced English as a defining characteristic. Cajun English has become a marker of group identity. One researcher asserts:

> In fact, the speaking of Cajun English is an important identity marker for both bilingual Cajuns and monolingual English-speaking Cajuns. . . . Some Cajuns are ashamed of their nonstandard English, but most are not. . . . Some individuals intensify their accents in situations where being a Cajun is an asset—for example when talking with outsiders who are known to be interested in Cajun culture or when taking part in public events that celebrate Cajun ethnicity. Male college students have told me that they consciously exaggerate their accents when vacationing at resorts outside of Acadiana, in order to attract the attention of non-Cajun women, who are allegedly fascinated by the Cajuns' unconventional style of speech. (Gutierrez 1992)

Others interpret the national spotlight as partially fueling the emergent dialect: "The public display of Cajun culture to outsiders—part of the tourist industry—reinforces the use of English as a carrier of Cajun identity" (Dubois and Horvath 1999:306).

In their sociolinguistic survey of Cajun English, Dubois and Horvath conducted interviews with self-identifying Cajuns from three generations (grouped as "older," "middle," and "younger"). They found that while some dialect markers were decreasing through time (meaning that the younger-generation speakers had fewer of these markers present in their speech than older-generation speakers), other markers showed an increase in usage or sustained usage. For example, rate of usage for dental stops in place of interdental fricatives ("thing" becomes "ting") was as high among younger speakers as among older speakers. In addition, the study identified that the subgroup of younger speakers most likely to use more Cajun dialect consisted of young males in wide social networks (Dubois and Horvath 1999). These are the people most often coming into contact with out-group people, so we can speculate that they are using their Cajun English to assert difference.

## DIALECT PERFORMANCE

Linguistic style variation, like phonetic variation, can be random and meaningless or patterned and meaningful. In the case of style, patterned variation can be read as a code referencing something outside the illocutionary force of the discourse itself. LePage and Tabouret-Keller (1985:14) characterize "linguistic behavior as a set of *acts of identity* in which people reveal both their personal identity and their search for social roles." Given that "Cajun" can entail so many meanings, it would seem one arduous task of this analysis would be to map specific linguistic traits onto the myriad of possible Cajun identities being encoded—that is, to discern the pattern. However, one-to-one mapping of linguistic behavior with "identity" or "positioning" (e.g., "distancing" or "solidarity") is problematic. Shifts in linguistic markers convey communicative intent, but that intent does not always reference the outside world or social relationships beyond the conversational group in a straightforward way. Sometimes a shift carries a particular, easily decoded meaning about social roles, and sometimes the exact same linguistic shift at a different juncture will convey a completely different meaning about social roles; will carry meaning about humor, performance, or speaker competence/repertoire; or will signal topic change or have some other pragmatic function.

> We cannot assume a fixed relationship between a social identity and the language of the utterance that evokes (or invokes) it; rather such relationships are themselves negotiated and constructed in the interaction, drawing on cultural resources located both inside and outside the interaction itself. . . . Social identities are made manifest through talk, not just through the actual language of 'code' used but also through the content and context. (Sebba and Wootten 1998:284)

For instance, during fieldwork I frequently heard "cher" inserted into English-language conversations. At times this signaled an assertion of group identity or a distancing from American English. At other times it marked the beginning of a joke, a habit of speech, or a signal of a close relationship between two interlocutors. Thus, even the use of the marker "cher," commonly used in performance genres to denote Cajunness, cannot always be reduced to a simple assertion of ethnicity. Pinning down the meaning in any given usage requires ethnographic data and native-speaker interpretation.

The Acadians in this study are active agents constructing meaning in their discourse. To use the word "shift" may imply that these styles are bounded entities, but they are not. It seems that the Acadians have at their disposal a large repertoire of possible linguistic forms—Southern, Standard American, Cajun English, and others. Their stories transcribed here are a type of poetics in which the speakers perform a full range of identities, drawing on their repertoire and their deep knowledge of the indexing possibilities carried by various linguistic markers. Meaning must be constantly interpreted in the context of each discourse event.

These stories are both casual conversation and examples of performances. First, the individuals know that they are being taped (indeed, they want to be taped), and second, they are performing on a topic that the researcher introduced. Much sociolinguistic research, seeking to arrive at some "truth" about "normal" speech, has searched for speech that is not self-conscious; performance speech, until recently, has been examined mostly by folklorists and anthropologists. That is beginning to change:

> The investigation of selfconscious speech, even overtly performative speech, seems essential in a research program in which stylistic variation is viewed as a resource for creating and projecting one's persona—that is, with performing an identity. (Schilling-Estes 2002:395)

Performing is itself a natural part of storytelling rounds, and these rounds are not fake, assumed, or put on for the researcher's benefit. While I lived in the hamlet where I conducted my research, at least once a week some subset of the people I worked with gathered at Claude's Country Store to swap stories. Although the topic on which they spoke did not occur naturally—I suggested it—it does not follow that the topic was unnatural. In fact, in a later conversation, one of the local people told me that having me as a catalyst provided a welcome opportunity to discuss ethnicity and identity (and to have a new audience for their performances). Thus, the participants were performing for me, but they were also performing for each other, as they often do.

Stories about meetings with outsiders are common, particularly vacation stories, although difficult to get on tape. In the retelling, the stories actually have several layers of performance. There is the performance put on for the outsiders during the original encounter. This encounter is then reenacted back home, and in the retelling, the storytellers "perform" their original performance. In this second performance, the storyteller re-creates the speech styles and mannerisms of the outsiders.

## THE STORYTELLING SESSION IN CLAUDE'S COUNTRY STORE

The storytelling/joke telling session transcribed here took place at Claude's Country Store, a small convenience store located on Bayou Terrebonne just down the bayou from Houma and up the bayou from Montegut. The store's clientele is mostly local, although they get a few tourists as well. I recorded there for about six weeks off and on. One of my first mornings there, a group of neighbors stopped in for coffee on their way to work and started asking me about what I was studying. When I explained that I was studying Cajun ethnicity, they immediately started telling me stories about what it's like to be labeled Cajun when you encounter the wider U.S. populace. The local residents in the store began recounting vacation stories with themes of how naive and insulting outsiders can be when they assume that Cajuns are ignorant folk. Then the talk turned to an insider topic about how *some* Cajuns really *are* ignorant folk. These stories were truly performances because my presence afforded the opportunity to tell or retell them.

The local residents stood in a semicircle and told their stories to each other. At its fullest, there were six in the group. I stood behind the circle listening and recording. Despite my position outside the circle, the performances were in part for my benefit. Because the stories started quickly, I didn't have a chance to ask permission to tape. When I asked permission at the laugh break, the first storyteller, obviously disappointed, said, "What? You weren't recording that?" The round consisted of several turns. Here I discuss three stories, one told before the tape recorder was on and two that I taped.

*"You wouldn't eat your dog, would you?"*

The first story was told by a man in his fifties, a first-language French speaker who lives life in English and raised his family in English. I'm calling him Moise. He told a story about standing in line at Disneyland. The lines were long and the people in line began chatting. When some people found out he and his wife were from Louisiana, these people asked if they were really Cajuns. He replied yes. And then a person asked him if it's true that Cajuns eat alligators. In his retelling, he feigned shock and said in a heavy accent, "Why no! We keep alligators for pets. You wouldn't eat your dog, would you?" The people shut up and left them alone. What came across in this story, as it was retold at Claude's Country Store, was indignation. Moise was not offended that someone assumed that he ate alligator or that Cajuns eat alligator. Some do; some don't. Rather, the offense was at the implied linkage he heard between eating habits and being odd, weird, or different from the American norm. Clearly, he heard the question to be interpreted not as "Could you please explain Cajun dietary habits" but as "Boy, Cajuns are really weird, disgusting, and low-class people who break food taboos." In U.S. culture, breaking food taboos, especially on meat, can be judged as class-aligned (think of the possum stew the Clampets would cook). In telling his joke, Moise was talking in his casual speech register, which is marked by a slight Cajun English dialect. In fact, when he performed his answer to the question "Are you really Cajuns," he continued to use his casual speech register. However, when he came to "Why no! We keep alligators for pets," he shifted to a greater intonational range (higher highs and lower lows), tenser vowels (more like French), a penultimate stress pattern, and a rising intonation on the end of the phrase "Why no." These shifts invoke French and signal Cajun English, which I and (I believe) the audience interpreted as a solidarity move. Moise was positioning himself as very Cajun. His response to the accusation of being a low-class Cajun was, in effect, Hell yes! And he proceeded to be the most down-the-bayou

Cajun he could be, and that Cajun was the one who put the Americans down and made them look plain silly. The audience in the store laughed heartily at the punch line, appreciated how the Cajun had made the Americans look dumb, and commiserated with each other about how people assume that Cajuns are backward.

The first performance of this joke by Moise (in Disneyland) could be interpreted as a performance that distances, while the second performance (in Claude's Country Store) could be interpreted as a solidarity move.[4]

### *"Gimme some of that gumbo"*

At this point I was able to turn on the tape recorder, and, after expressing disappointment in my not taping the first story, Moise immediately launched into another. While on vacation, he and his wife stopped in a restaurant.[5]

> I said give me some gumbo also ( ) shrimp gumbo ( ) she says ( )
> uh is that foreign food? they said—well the owner of the place says no \ ,
> he's talking about—he's from Louisiana \ ,
> that's Louisiana food he's talking about \ .
> she didn't—she actually didn't know what the heck I was talking about \ .
> she thought I was talking about some foreign country or something \ .

In this story Moise turns the tables on the rest of America by walking into a restaurant and ordering a dish that, until recently, was mostly unknown outside of Louisiana. His point here is the ignorance of the restaurant waitress who didn't even know that gumbo was American ("She thought I was talking about some foreign country or something"). He told this story quickly and mostly used his "normal" speech voice, even when performing the clueless waitress. His performative markers focused on his pause after "she says" (for effect) and the careful parallel lengths of the phrases, reflecting both poetics and personal style. The content of this story carried his assertion of Cajun identity.

People laughed, commiserated, clucked their tongues, shook their heads. By the end of this story the group was in solidarity, united as Cajuns in viewing the deep levels of general American ignorance.

### *"I would like to say this though"*

Then a woman I'm calling Clothilde told a story. She set up her story as contrasting with the previous story by saying, "I would like to say this, though."

The contrast she called her audience's attention to was her stance toward Cajun identity. (Her opening phrase also functions as a structural segment to shift to take the floor, and as a poetic device to introduce balance to the conversation.) Afterward Moise jumped in with a supporting story, and Claude, the storekeeper, offered his words of support. In Clothilde's story I've used International Phonetic Alphabet characters for the occurrence (or lack) of linguistic markers such as nasalization, stress, and dental stops vs. interdental fricatives. Nasalization is marked by a tilde (~); stress is marked by a small apostrophe ('); and intonation curves are marked by slanted lines (/ \). The symbol "ð" represents the first sound in the Standard American English pronunciation of the word *this* and "θ" represents the first sound in the standard pronunciation of the word *thing*. Dental stops are marked by a little symbol ( ̪) under the consonant. Lines are broken into phrases.

**Clothilde:** I would like to say this though ( )<br>
ðɪs ðo \

my mother went to the dentist's office one day<br>
məðɚ ðə dɪnɪsts

and she was sitting down and this Cajun lady walked in \<br>
ðɪs

and she was holding the side of her mouth,<br>
ðə

and she was saying, —oh yi yai, oh, yi yai \

the secretary says, the secretary says ma'am / \ ( )<br>
ðə ðə

can I help you? /

and she said oh cher ( ) she said \<br>
ʃæ̃

I need to see that dentist. ( )<br>
ni tə si ðæ̃ 'dɪnɪs / \

she said well do you need an extraction?

oh no cher that thing needs to be pulled out<br>
o: nõ ʃæ̃ d̪æ tin nidz təbi 'puldau?

(LAUGHTER)

**Moise:** I was, I was telling Ezoleen I went to

Dr. Alexander had a, had, uh,

( ) talk last night at the hospital
ðə

( ) on cancer, prostate cancer.

( ) so I had gone to Dr. Collins years back

and Mabel was sitting outside in the waiting room

and this old lady from down the bayou was talking to her,
ðɪs

a real old French woman from down around Chauvin somewhere.

So she asked Mabel, "Say what you in here for?"

Mabel says I'm not in here

says my husband's in here

says uh well what's wrong with him?
wɪθ

well says uh he's got prostate trouble

oh she said mais cher I got that too \ .
ʃi sɛd meᴵ ʃæ̃ ɑy gɑ dæ̃ 'tŭ

(LAUGHTER)

**Moise:** Isn't it true ( )

I was telling that,

I was telling that to ooh boy last night I just

I was telling that to Wanda Lecompte—Mrs.

Lecompte from over on the bayou she said

oh boy that's you call a hypochondriac

(LAUGHTER)

**Claude:** She probably didn't know what the hell it was.

(LAUGHTER)

In this excerpt, Clothilde draws on her linguistic repertoire to project three varieties. The first variety is her casual speaking voice, which (like Moise's) is a light Cajun English dialect. In setting up the story Clothilde uses interdental fricatives and an English stress pattern. However, she abruptly shifts to perform the voice of the "Cajun lady" using the heavily marked lexical items "Oh yi yai, oh yi yai." That shift is marked by a change in voice quality and a wider range of intonation curves. She then abruptly shifts back to her storytelling voice. The third persona she creates is the secretary. Again her voice quality changes to a type of crispness and she says (in slightly hypercorrect vowels), "Can I help you?" In portraying the response to the secretary's question, she again performs the "Cajun lady" voice, with another marked lexical item, "cher," which is heavily nasalized. In addition to voice quality changes, she uses a flat intonation pattern on the Cajun lady's "I need to see that dentist," putting stress on the last word in the phrase (a French language pattern). That same line is marked by the dropping of the final consonants in "need," "that," and "dentist" as well as the nasalization on "that." Note that the speaker retained her voiced interdental fricative. She next switches back to the crisp secretary voice ("well do you need an extraction?"), which she follows with her heaviest Cajun performance ("oh no cher that thing needs to be pulled out"). She has nasalization on "no" and "cher." She shifts from an interdental to a dental stop on "thing." She has marked liaison between words "that thing," "thing needs," and "pulled out." Again, she has flat intonation except for the last word of the phrase.

For his part, Moise relates a conversation between his wife and "this old lady from down the bayou," "a real old French woman from down around Chauvin somewhere." These location indicators are important because in Terrebonne Parish the farther "down the bayou" you live, the farther you are from town. Local people associate backwardness and retention of French characteristics with being "down the bayou." Moise does not use the label "Cajun." He clearly specifies that this woman is "other" because she is a "French" lady. He also points out that she comes from "down the bayou." Moise puts on exaggerated Cajun English dialect to tell how the woman talks: "Oh, mais cher, I got [dat] too." He adds French words, shifts to a phrase-final stress pattern, adds nasalization, shortens and tenses his vowels, and changes his interdental to a stop.

## CONCLUSION

Through these three stories, the group of five or so people created a consensus about their identity that we can see by their general agreement—at the same moments as a group they share laughter and disbelief. They tell stories that reinforce each other's points and offer support through body posture and full attention. By the end of this conversation, I am convinced, they have all shared something meaningful about their identities, have reaffirmed something. Because I am an outsider, the specific nature of this identity is not clear to me. I played parts of this tape for them and then, in the weeks to come, for others who were willing to help me. Most puzzling for me was their willingness to both defend Cajuns and make sport of Cajuns for an outsider. But I learned that their identities are complex: Cajun, Southern, American. As Clothilde ably demonstrated in her story, they can put on or project any of these identities through linguistic manipulation. However, they are not just engaging in what Rampton (1995) refers to as "crossing" over to other cultures and borrowing identities. They also *own* these identities. That is, they can use Standard English or Southern English as a variety they control if the situation calls for it, not just in parody. Because the shifts are so dramatic and entertaining and because *Cajun* is foregrounded, it is easy to see this round in the light of assertions about ethnic identity. But after talking with the participants afterward, letting them listen to the tape, and letting others in the community listen to the tape, I have come to think that any interpretation must be more complex. Clearly, the early stories were directed toward me with the subtext of my research: these were warnings about what kinds of data I might get if I started with the assumption that Acadians are stupid. Later, the storytelling took on its own momentum. There was not only a sense of positioning in Clothilde's story, but a poetic discourse move to create balance. Their exaggerations suggest a love of language play and storytelling. This type of manipulation is artful and poetic and takes skill and practice.

Recognizing the other possible readings, I would like to focus on ethnic positioning. Clearly, these stories are full of ambivalences about the ethnic group *Cajun*. This study shows individuals performing exaggerated types of what they perceive to be their own ethnic accent, or rather the packaged commodity of *Cajun English*. In some of these cases, "Cajun" becomes "Other," a clear form of distancing.

The performers allow their audience to get the joke and its subtext by competently switching styles. In one round Moise positions himself in solidarity with Cajun ethnicity by using exaggerated Cajun English. In another story, Moise uses exaggerated Cajun English to distance himself from that same identity. Because being Cajun is such a salient feature in the region in which these people live, and throughout Louisiana and to some degree all over the United States, these people constantly confront the issue of identification. As European Americans, they have the option of ethnic identity in a way not available to people classified as nonwhite. They can choose whether or not to identify as Cajun. With other in-group members, they can also choose, through discourse strategies such as dialect manipulation, to what degree they are going to be Cajun.

The Louisiana Acadians represented in this study used dialect exaggeration in discourse as one way to negotiate the tricky territory of self-positioning as a "Cajun" or an "unhyphenated American." Exaggeration shifts are a particularly sophisticated tool for encoding social meaning about identity among a people, such as the Cajuns, who must negotiate situations of culture change and negotiate movement between cultural worlds. One reason such shifts are effective is that one's positioning is easily altered, even within one discourse event.

A person cannot analyze what is actually being communicated between the group members in this storytelling session without knowing basic ethnographic information about the group. To understand the group's rules of conduct and to grasp the complete ambivalences, it is necessary to know the history of power and ethnic relationships (for instance, why other Americans are able to make what seem to be negative assumptions about Cajuns with impunity). The ambivalence in these stories lies along several axes of tension: between wanting to be an ethnic Cajun but not wanting to suffer from the social stigma of being a "backward Cajun"; between wanting to be considered white, mainstream Americans and yet not wanting to forfeit a cultural heritage that lends depth and meaning to life; and between the desire to claim a sense of community and the need to distance themselves from that same community.

## NOTES

1. Acadian identity and race do not always align in a straightforward manner. All of the Acadians who participated in this storytelling round also classify themselves as "white"; however, there are some individuals in Louisiana who self-identify as both African American and Acadian. See Brasseaux 1992, Henry 1998, Trépanier 1991, and Walton 2003 for discussions of racial identity among Acadians.

2. Although "Cajun" and "Acadian" are today considered socially acceptable English words to use as descriptors for the people who originally came from Nova Scotia and settled in Louisiana, many social activists and, in fact, most French speakers in southern Louisiana prefer the French form "Acadien" and its abbreviation "cadien." Some activists prefer the written form of "cadjin" because it more clearly reflects the pronunciation of most Cajun French speakers. The history of the forms and the positioning of social activists is laid out in Henry 1998. I use both *Cajun* and *Acadian,* following the norms in books such as Ancelet, Edwards, and Pitre 1991.

3. While French is being revived, it is often not Acadian French that the younger generation chooses to speak. Cajun French remains an endangered language (Amanda LaFleur, personal communication 1998).

4. Thanks to Margaret Bender for this idea.

5. Notes on transcription: Speech is transcribed as lines to capture intonational contours. Parentheses, ( ), indicate a pause, and a back slash, \, indicates a falling intonation pattern.

## REFERENCES


Alba, Richard D. 1990. *Ethnic Identity: The Transformation of White America.* New Haven: Yale University Press.

Ancelet, Barry Jean, Jay Edwards, and Glen Pitre. 1991. *Cajun Country.* Jackson: University Press of Mississippi.

Brasseaux, Carl. 1992. *Acadian to Cajun: Transformation of a People, 1803–1977.* Jackson: University Press of Mississippi.

Dorman, James H. 1984. Louisiana's Cajuns: A Case Study of Ethnic Group Revitalization. *Social Science Quarterly* 65:1043–57.

Dubois, Sylvie, and Barbara Horvath. 1998. Let's tink about dat: Interdental Fricatives in Cajun English. *Language Variation and Change* 10:246–61.

———. 1999. When the music changes, you change too: Gender and Language Change in Cajun English. *Language Variation and Change* 11:287–313.

Gutierrez, Paige. 1992. *Cajun Foodways.* Jackson: University Press of Mississippi.

Henry, Jacques. 1998. From Acadien to Cajun to Cadien: Ethnic Labelization and Construction of Identity. *Journal of American Ethnic History* 17(4):29–63.

Henry, Jacques M., and Carl L. Bankston III. 1999. Louisiana Cajun Ethnicity: Symbolic or Structural? *Sociological Spectrum* 19(2):223–49.

Le Page, R. B., and Andrée Tabouret-Keller. 1985. *Acts of Identity.* Cambridge: Cambridge University Press.

Pennfield, Joyce, and Jacob Ornstein-Galicia. 1985. *Chicano English: An Ethnic Contact Dialect.* Philadelphia: John Benjamin.

Rampton, Ben. 1995. *Crossing: Language and Ethnicity among Adolescents*. New York: Longman.

Schilling-Estes, Natalie. 2002. Investigating Stylistic Variation. In *The Handbook of Language Variation and Change,* ed. J. K. Chambers, Peter Trudgill, and Natalie Schilling-Estes, pp. 375–401. Malden, Mass.: Blackwell.

Scott, Ann, ed. 1992. Cajun Vernacular English: Informal English in French Louisiana. Special issue of the *Louisiana English Journal.*

Sebba, Mark, and Tony Wootten. 1998. We, They, and Identity: Sequential versus Identity-Related Explanation in Code-Switching. In *Code-Switching in Conversation: Language, Interaction, and Identity,* ed. Peter Auer, pp. 262–86. New York: Routledge.

Trépanier, Cécyle. 1991. The Cajunization of French Louisiana: The Forging of a Regional Identity. *Geographic Journal* 157(2):161–71.

Walton, Shana. 1994. Flat Speech and Cajun Ethnic Identity in Terrebonne Parish, Louisiana. Ph.D. dissertation, Tulane University, New Orleans.

———. 2003. The Coonass Phenomenon: Choosing Race and Class over Ethnicity. In *Signifying Serpents and Mardi Gras Runners: Representing Identity in Selected Souths,* ed. Celeste Ray and Luke Eric Lassiter. Southern Anthropological Society Proceedings, No. 36. Athens: University of Georgia Press.

Waters, Mary C. 1990. *Ethnic Options: Choosing Identities in America*. Berkeley: University of California Press.

# Identity, Hybridity, and Linguistic Ideologies of Racial Language in the Upper South

*Anita Puckett*

Recent scholarship on the "discourses of whiteness" has foregrounded how anthropological approaches to linguistic ideologies can make visible seemingly invisible or covert racially identifying functions of language in use (Bucholtz and Trechter 2002). By considering the "way in which people conceive of links between linguistic forms and social phenomena" (Irvine and Gal 2000:37) from the perspective of race, that is, their linguistic ideologies of racial language, this scholarship makes clear how race and conditions of white access, privilege, and power emerge from sociolinguistic interaction to become a constitutive force in reproducing a culturally constructed racial elite. Therefore, the major goal of this scholarship has been to "characterize more precisely, and thereby to productively attack, the culture of racism that has the production of whiteness as a central project" (Hill 2001:83).

This paper builds on such scholarship by examining how discursive practices used by Melungeon and Scotch Irish identity groups in the upland South, also known as southern Appalachia, ascribe value to the names they use to identify themselves. I assert that these names, or ethnonyms, circulate in the economic sense of being distributed into diverse socioeconomic and political-economic contexts. In this case, however, they circulate within the various oral and written discourse practices that constitute the verbal repertoire (Hymes 1972) of those using the term. In so doing, these ethnonyms acquire various valued properties, which may be positive or negative, that function to give or deny access to white privilege, power, and prestige. By "value," I mean the "degree to which *objects* are desired, particularly, as measured by how much others are willing to give up to get them" (Graeber 2001:1, italics mine). In offering this general definition of "value," I am purposefully indefinite so that how "value" is constituted emerges from the discursive meanings created or reproduced in verbal interactions.

In making these claims concerning material properties of ethnonyms, I am conforming to Silverstein's argument that ethnonyms can have some object properties in which they represent a "culturally-local system of validated ownership, alienability, and usufruct according to a social understanding of what holds instances of use of language together" (Silverstein 1984:1). At the same time, I am also asserting that certain components of language, in this case, names that identify cultural groups (ethnonyms) in English, can assume certain economic properties of objects—and circulate within groups assuming a range of exchange-like functions similar to emblems or heirlooms (e.g., surnames), goods (e.g., the use of "Irish" to obtain political access), or even commodities (e.g., the buying or selling of "hillbilly" or "redneck" in mediated forms such as joke collections or bumper stickers), much like material objects. In so doing, I am arguing that the boundaries between language and tangible objects are not clear-cut, but permeable, "leaky" as it were (after Hill 1995). By implication, I am also asserting that a rigorous theoretical approach to linguistic ideology and its contributions to an understanding of the political-economic implications of racial language must include a theoretically rigorous understanding of how language and economic relations are constituted.

To assert that ethnonyms can function as circulating objects, I also argue that the textual and contextual significations created or, more commonly, reproduced through these circulations construct a complex of meanings that infuse the ethnonym with racially loaded emblematic and totemic force (cf. Urban 1981). With repeated usage in similar discursive practices, the ethnonym becomes embedded with culturally validated meanings so that it has the capacity to evoke strong emotive and group-significant importance apart from a specific discursive context, not unlike the meaning properties of a valued material object. These meanings also function to assign individuals positions within or outside of the group referenced by the name. In addition, these meanings complexly interconnect the ethnonym and the discursive instance in which it appears to other discursive texts and contexts through evocative and relational entailments or links. In this process of linking to other linguistic practices, they conform to Irvine's insight that a specific speech event and the participants in it recollect or directly index (or point to) other past, future, hypothetical, and even avoided communicative acts

(Irvine 1996:135). That is, when interlocutors use an ethnonym, whether directly (face to face) or in a mediated form (via print or an electronic medium), they connect it, its presupposed significations, and the immediate event in which it is imbedded to others past or anticipated and to the communicative practices that by memory, convention, or habitus are associated with them. Consequently, a full understanding of the political-economic implications of these ethnonyms is not possible without an ethnographically informed understanding of how these circulation regimes interconnect to assign these interlinking meanings. When this understanding is possible, then insights into how these linkages help shape racial language will be clearer. Issues of ongoing racism and the cultural construction of racial disempowerment can then be more accurately addressed.

By "ethnographically informed," I refer to those data obtained through linguistic anthropological methods of participant observation in which researchers engage in the full range of communicative practices extant in a speech community to obtain as full an understanding of the semantic, pragmatic, and metapragmatic significations of the communicative repertoire as possible (cf. Duranti 1997:84–102). By "repertoire," I refer not just to the grammatical resources of a speech community, but also to the distinctive discursive, participant framework, contextual, and nonverbal elements that define a "communicative practice" (Hymes 1972) such as praying, storytelling, conversation, and instructing. By "pragmatic" and "metapragmatic," I am referring to Silverstein's (1979; 1993; 1996; 2001) formulation of indexical relationships to context and to metacontext. "Pragmatic" relationships are context specific and represent how a sign, such as the pronoun "you," points to something else in the event, in this case, the person addressed. "Metapragmatic" relationships, as I am using the term here, are glosses or other ways of coding speech or action into more general frameworks, categories, or types. For example, phrases such as "I'm just joking" or "he's preaching at us" function in part as metapragmatic indexes categorizing the event in which they are uttered.

## APPALACHIAN IDENTITIES

I have been engaged in ethnographic research on two identity groups, the Melungeons and the Scotch Irish, in three Appalachian communities, one in southeastern Kentucky, one in eastern Tennessee, and the third in southwestern Virginia. I have also collected structured interviews, oral histories, and ethnohistorical materials from other sources, including the Melungeon Heritage Association (MHA) and the Scotch-Irish Society of the United States of America.

The MHA and the Melungeon identity movement gained momentum in the late 1990s after the publication of Brent Kennedy's popular autobiographical account concerning his Melungeon ancestry and heritage (Kennedy 1994). The movement is centered in the Appalachian regions of far southwestern Virginia and eastern Tennessee, where the term was originally most common and where Dr. Kennedy lives. Nevertheless, much of the communication among its members and to general publics is mediated, occurring virtually through chat rooms, e-mail discussion lists, and Web sites, through publications such as magazine articles, newspaper features, or popular-audience-focused books, or through radio broadcasts (e.g., *All Things Considered* 1997), educational television videos (e.g., Martin 1997), or compact disk recordings (Winkler 1999) that have received regional, national, and international attention on public broadcast television and radio and through academic venues such as classes and symposia. Most individuals who self-identify as Melungeon are white-collar or upper-middle-class professionals who are exploring their "roots" or are experiencing epiphanic revelations concerning gaps in their understanding of their family background or identity.

Historically, the epithet "Melungeon" was an exonym, that is, a term used primarily by nonmembers to deride and stigmatize those presumed to have been of mixed race ancestry, usually presumed by academics to have been Native American or African American and northern European. The Melungeon Heritage Association, beginning with Kennedy's book, has disputed this mixed "race" origin and argues instead for Turkish, Portuguese, Spanish, Jewish, and other southern European or Mediterranean ancestry. No distinctive or diagnostic material artifacts or linguistic forms have been recorded to support either claim, although provocative anecdotes and recollections circulate in personal oral and written accounts (cf. Sovine 1983), and enough historical and archaeological evidence exists to suggest that a "tri-racial" argument is too simplistic (Everett 1999).

The word "Melungeon" occurred primarily in far southwestern Virginia, eastern Tennessee, and far southeastern Kentucky. The first known recorded usage was in 1813 in the records of a church in Scott County, Virginia (Everett 1999). Given its stigmatization, systematic and conscious efforts were and are made to erase "Melungeon" from the local lexicon within those communities with high Melungeon populations. This erasure has resulted in "Melungeon" having extremely limited discursive circulation in these areas, and no positive value. As a result, tension exists between these communities and the MHA members or other peripheral Melungeon-affirming individuals who use the word frequently and assign positive value to it (Puckett 2001).

Contrastively, the MHA and its concomitant identity movement has as one of its goals to invest "Melungeon" with positive status through empowered and privileged recognition of the mixed "heritage" of its members. If successful, the MHA will elevate "Melungeon" to be a source of symbolic capital that would grant an image of respectability and a reputation of competence to its members (Bourdieu 1984:291). It is to these processes of positive valuation that I now turn.

Within the restricted face-to-face interactions in "Melungeon"-familiar communities, the term "Melungeon" has been reintroduced into ancestor narratives, genealogy discussions, and in "just talk" and "gossip" concerning the reputability and character of various movement leaders. It has appeared in limited ways in prayer, witnessing, and other religious practices. Some teachers and professors have also incorporated it into various educational contexts in regional K–12 classrooms and at various community and regional colleges. Annual "unions" or "gatherings" also provide organized venues where the ethnonym is validated through lectures, familial or community narratives, genealogical discussions and kinship talk, praying, quoting scripture, testifying, conversation (or "just talkin"), and other practices that foreground identity and group membership (Puckett 2001).

The lectures presented at the gatherings are given by those introduced by their scholarly titles (doctor, professor, teacher), who present in speech conforming to Standard American English grammar, and who present their material as informational and accurate. Many of those attending these reunions either are not Appalachian English speakers or were originally but have also embraced Standard American English speaking practices and the linguistic ideologies of literacy they reproduce. These members are unlike primary Appalachian English speakers who commonly assign negative value to these scholarly forms of talk, assigning the metapragmatic gloss of "educated talk" spoken by those who "think they're better than we are." Instead, the members assign high value to the scholarly forms, as "discourses of truth" (after Hill 2001: 262–63) that validate a specific Melungeon ancestry, history, and culture.

Consequently, the speakers and audiences at these presentations seemingly reproduce the participant frameworks and speaking practices that scholarly presentations presuppose. Generally fully or partially reading from a written text or notes, one person utters a presentation from behind a podium to a quiet audience. The presentation indexes the participant framework of "the lecture" in which the one controlling the ebb and flow of talk is assumed to have intellectual "authority," "knowledge," and "experience" in textual matters and the subject matter the texts reference, not only in relation to the immediate audience, but also in relation to audiences who have access to the videotapes or written representations (Goffman 1981:167). These presentations, then, in which "Melungeon" occurs frequently as an informational topic couched within Standard American English grammar, elevate what was an epithet to the level of scholarly treatment within a discourse practice that is seemingly similar in form and function with one of the highest forms of "whiteness" (cf. Bucholtz 2001).

Written variants of these lectures, and other texts conforming to the informational or argumentative discursive framework of scholarship, interconnect these instances of lectures and the settings in which they occur through various similarities of style and referential content (cf. Irvine and Gal 2000). That is, printed and online reports concerning Melungeon "research" are offered in stylistic, grammatical, and discursive form similar to conventional scholarly texts. For example, the Melungeon Heritage Association's Web site's FAQ (Frequently Asked Questions) section reads as follows:

> 1. WHO ARE THE MELUNGEONS?
> The Melungeons are a sizable mixed-ethnic population spread throughout the southeastern United States and into southern Ohio and Indiana. While the term "Melungeon" is most commonly applied to those group members living in eastern Kentucky, southwestern Virginia, eastern Tennessee, and southern West Virginia, related mixed-ancestry populations also include the Carmel Indians of southern Ohio, the Brown People of Kentucky, the Guineas of West Virginia, the We-Sorts of Maryland, the Nanticoke-Moors of Delaware, the Cubans and Portuguese of North Carolina, the Turks and Brass Ankles of South Carolina, and the Creoles and Redbones of Alabama, Mississippi, and Louisiana. Probable Native American kinship for the various groups includes the Algonquin tribes of eastern and central Virginia, as well as the Lumbees, Monacans, Saponi, Catawba, Cherokee, and Muskogee/Creek tribes of the deeper south. . . .
>
> 2. WHAT IS A MELUNGEON?
> A growing body of evidence supports the now centuries-old Melungeon claim to be variously of Portuguese, Turkish, Moorish, Arabic, and Jewish

origin, mixed with Native Americans. Oral tradition, cultural evidence, linguistics, and physical phenotypes point toward a strong Mediterranean and Middle Eastern component among most of the Melungeon related populations. Genetic and medical evidence confirm the same probable linkages, regardless of how it came to be. A 1990 gene frequency study (Guthrie, Tennessee Anthropologist, Spring 1990) utilizing 177 Melungeon blood samples showed no significance [*sic*] differences between east Tennessee and southwestern Virginia Melungeons and populations in Spain, Portugal, North Africa, Malta, Cyprus, Greece, Iran and Iraq, and the Levant (Turkey, Syria, Lebanon). Diseases identified in the Melungeon population include thallasemia, Behcet's Syndrome, Machado-Joseph (Azorean) Disease, sarcoidosis, and Familial Mediterranean Fever. More than 1000 Melungeon and related Native American terms have been preliminarily linked with Ottoman period Turkish and Arabic words with identical pronunciations and meaning. Even the long-standing mystery term "Melungeon" is itself pronounced identically to the Arabic and Turkish terms "Melun jinn" and "Melun can" meaning "cursed soul." . . . Importantly, "Melungeon" was NOT, is NOT a racial or ethnic group.

From the beginning, the term was applied to a diverse group of primarily sixteenth-century Mediterranean/Middle Eastern/Central Asian immigrants who suffered great prejudice and united in an effort to survive encroaching Anglo-American racism and depopulation, but which later splintered into numerous ethnic enclaves in the continuing effort to survive. While most modern day Melungeon groups have preserved at least some cultural artifacts of their earliest population characteristics, each group has gone its own way. For this reason, some Melungeon groups and individuals have totally assimilated into the American mainstream, while others cling to, variously, predominantly Turkish, or Portuguese, or Native American, or African, or European roots. . . .

4. WHAT IS THE IMPORTANCE OF THE STORY?
First, it is important to accurately understand the truth of how we developed as a Nation, including the challenges we faced. . . .

Second, it is important to understand who we are as individuals and as "communities" of people. Self-identity and self-respect must come before respect for others and love of Nation. Melungeons and other mixed-ethnic groups have historically been told that they MUST fit into ONE of the single racial categories offered via the census. This is ahistorical, asinine, even irrational. The results of such narrow-mindedness can be seen today, where

> mixed-ancestry children have generally been forced to self-identify with one parent only when the child naturally identifies with BOTH parents. For this reason—the right of self-identification and dignity—this story is important.
>
> Third, the story of the Melungeons is important because it shows the previously obscured and often vehemently denied human kinship between us all. The tangled web of the Melungeons and their mixed-ethnic cousins demonstrates the human family's connections linking brown to white to red to yellow to black, and also of Americans in general to not only Englishmen, but to Turks, Jews, Spaniards, and yes, even Iraqis. . . . There may indeed be a lesson for the whole world in the story of one of the most disparaged people on earth: the Melungeons.[1]

This text, by its placement on the MHA Web site, receives the indexical value of the "official" (or Association) stance toward these issues. In terms of its linguistic ideological positioning, however, this site is much more complex.

This Web page assumes the question/answer format of one style of academic writing, uses Standard American English grammatical forms, is organized into paragraphs conforming to conventional essay style, and incorporates factually referential language framed in indicative sentences relying heavily on Greco-Latinate polysyllabic lexicon with words such as "disparaged" and "asinine." In this way, it conforms to the conventions of the kinds of scholarly texts characterizing academic writing. Indeed, this text, and various versions of this page, circulate and evoke metacommentary on Melungeon e-mail discussion lists and Web sites, at annual gatherings, and in classroom discussion, even at university levels. Through these patterns of circulation, the claims this page asserts are considered truthful by many members and nonmembers, and as a result, "Melungeon" is acquiring value as an object of scholarly legitimization. At the same time, "Melungeon" is also circulating in extensive genealogical and kinship discourse. Thus, the term is weaving together these two regimes of recognized white identity in ways that elevate and potentially legitimate "Melungeon" as a verbal object of value (Puckett 2001). In this way, those claiming the "right" to use the term are becoming a group of related people with a history, at least to some publics. From this perspective, it is becoming "white."

Nevertheless, this text is nonconforming to academic discourse first through the absence of conventionalized, or presupposing, indexes (Silverstein 1996) that interconnect one text to another or to expectations of how scholarly research is presented. Among them is the lack of documentation to support the veracity of the assertions. For example, the statement "A growing body of evidence supports the now centuries-old Melungeon claim" offers no citations or other forms of reference to this alleged body of evidence, therefore violating scholarly conventions of situating claims within the available scholarship. Second is absence of specific "factual," or referentially verifiable, support for assertions such as "Oral tradition, cultural evidence, linguistics, and physical phenotypes point toward a strong Mediterranean and Middle Eastern component among most of the Melungeon related populations." A third is that definitions of key concepts such as "ethnic group" and "mixed-ethnic population" are absent, leaving readers to infuse these abstract phrases with their own diverse meanings.

Furthermore, the text violates creative, or idiosyncratic, indexical relationships that readers of scholarly literature commonly bring to the referential functions of the discourse as well. For example, linguistic scholars reading the section on Native American/Turkish/Arabic lexical parallels (under "What is a Melungeon?") are likely to be off put by its failure to provide the kinds of scholarly analysis or links to the types of methodologies they expect to encounter in valid scholarly writing. Without such links, or entailments, such scholars tend to reject the assertion of linguistic relationships. Indeed, many scholars have attacked these arguments online, in print, and in person because of these metapragmatic violations (e.g., Henige 1998; Everett 1999). As a result of these violations, the linguistic processes valuating "Melungeon" are not being acknowledged among many Melungeon-familiar local residents, most scholars, or even much of the general public. For these audiences, "Melungeon" and the political-economic relations that have created its circulation in discourse do not make it "white" and empowered.

Assuming that the writer of this material is simply unfamiliar with the academic conventions of the essay would be too easily dismissive of the impact these assertions have had on Melungeons, general audiences interested in "Melungeon" as a topic, and educators or students who surf the Web for Melungeon information. Nor would it account for an MHA officer's response at an annual gathering that he doesn't care whether academics and others condemn Melungeon research because "Melungeon" is "ours." Nor does a dismissive stance acknowledge the politically positioned nature of all systems of ideas about the functions of language, or their linguistic ideologies, including those sustaining academic scholarship (Irvine and Gal 2000:36).

The MHA Web site should be examined not just as a text indexing prestige and empowerment through its similarity with scholarly rhetoric that, in turn, adds to the value of its users' symbolic capital. The site also evokes the significations indexed and symbolized by Appalachian Protestant religious doctrinal discursive practices (Puckett 2000) as well as Protestant practices in other regions of the United States. The text conforms to certain types of religious tracts common in American Protestant churches, particularly those catechismal tracts answering specific doctrinal or belief questions. For these types of materials, authority, prestige, and value are complexly constituted by the tracts' use in Sunday schools, prayer meetings, Bible meetings, home worship gatherings, and private meditation, that is, communicative events that legitimate them as representations of the beliefs of communities of saints. From this perspective, issues of factual substantiation and rigorous application of scholarly research methods are not only irrelevant, but potentially blasphemous.

The Melungeon text brings to mind many of the same assertions as do doctrinal tracts. For example, the sentence "Importantly, 'Melungeon' was NOT, is NOT a racial or ethnic group" has the elocutionary force of a statement of belief. Similarly, the sentence "For this reason—the right of self-identification and dignity—this story is important" also asserts moral authority through the use of "right of self-identification" and "dignity," both deontic principles of Protestantism. Therefore, the truth value of the text need not be referentially or historically validated, just as scriptural interpretations need not be, because they are matters of belief agreed upon by church or congregation.

Consequently, the character, the persona, of the disembodied author of this text asserts four major participant roles that are laminated one on another: that of a Melungeon, that of a Melungeon Heritage Association leader, that of an expert on Melungeon historical and cultural issues (a "scholar" if you will), and that of a sacredly privileged speaker (a "preacher" if you will). The text, then, is a discursive hybrid, overlapping authoritative discursive practices characteristic of different personae, two of which (preacher and scholar) are highly empowered, shifting according to various speech communities' systems of valuation, and two of which (Melungeon and MHA leader) are historically stigmatized, disempowered, or simply dismissed. The linguistic ideological significations of prestigious and authoritative language constituted by this merger of forms, functions, and meanings are then disputational, subject to readers' deconstruction according to the discursive practice or practices with which they associate (or metapragmatically index) it.

In contrast, the ethnonym "Scotch Irish," unlike "Melungeon," is well known, circulates widely across multiple verbal repertoires in numerous speech communities and social strata, and has achieved high prestige value in many subregions of the United States, particularly in the upland South. For this region, the discursive texts and contexts in which "Scotch Irish" creates or reproduces its value generally reference genealogical, family historical, or American sociopolitical historical matters, particularly of the eighteenth century. Vigorous debates sometimes involving hundreds of participants over phrase etymology, groups referenced and geographical locales of origin (Ulster Scots of Northern Ireland or Scots in Scotland and Northern Ireland), and appropriate spelling ("Scotch-Irish" versus "Scotch Irish" versus "Scots Irish") periodically appears in casual conversations among group members, at the many local and regional festivals celebrating Scotch or Scotch Irish heritage, and in all forms of mediated communication, from e-mail discussion lists to academic scholarship (cf. Montgomery 2002). In revealing the strength and scope of those claiming use or ownership rights to the term, these debates verify the vitality and established positive value of "Scotch Irish" (and its variants) as an ethnonym referencing an established, privileged, and empowered group.

Several organizations formally and legally function as heritage preservation entities. The one with the most "official" status is the Scotch-Irish Society of the United States of America. The Scotch-Irish Society, in contrast to the MHA, is a nationally recognized heritage association established in 1889 to preserve "Scotch-Irish history, [keep] alive the *esprit de corps* of the Scotch-Irish as a people, [and promote] social intercourse and fraternal feeling among its members" (Scotch-Irish Society). Similar to the MHA, it is the official organization for those affirming a Scotch-Irish heritage, ancestry, or ethnicity, which is generally considered to be determined by one's genealogy and surname. Membership is composed of those who consider themselves or are considered to be white.

Consequently, the term "Scotch Irish," again unlike "Melungeon," has established value similar to an heirloom in that it is inalienably inherited, can have enormous sentimental and emotional value, and grants rights of access to lineage-based social, political, and economic privileges at local, regional, and national levels. Also like an heirloom, individuals and families can disclaim "Scotch Irish" as their own. In this sense, "Scotch Irish" functions as a good that can be dispossessed or discarded (cf. Silverstein 1996; see also Urban 1981 and Parmentier 1985). Regardless of how potential owners approach possessing it, however, "Scotch Irish" circulates among those white populations who use it as an identifier of their heritage group.

In a short scene recorded by C-SPAN in Chesnee, South Carolina, on January 12, 2002, one can see the process of reproducing established value. Here at the site of the Cowpens National Battlefield, Dr. Walter Edgar, historian and author of *Partisans and Redcoats,* had spoken to an audience of about twenty local residents, all white and all middle-aged or older. After his lecture, a local woman (here designated LocWoman) spoke from the audience:[2]

**Edgar:** Yes ma'am (turning and semi-pointing to woman in right corner of front row.)

**LocWoman:** I have a personal story about Ferguson's grave.
My great grandmother who was born in . uhm . .
1870.

**Edgar:** Uh-huh (softly)

**LocWoman:** And lived to be ninety-nine years old. She was a Scotch Irish 'Carter from this area.
Uhm . as a child she would take me to Fer- Ferguson's grave every year.
She considered it a 'pilgrimage to go there
And throw a 'stone
On this dirty rotten scoundrel's 'grave

[audience laughter]

**LocWoman:** [Which her 'father and her 'grandfather had taken 'her on this pilgrimage all of 'her life.]
'Now the 'sign says
To put a stone for some politically correct reason

[audience laughter]

[Not (unintelligible) not]
She took me 'there to throw the stone.
As she had been taught
All of 'her life.
Because he had been so horrible
That he still needed that stone thrown on his grave.

**Edgar:** Ahh . ah . without
without revealing your age ma'am
When were you growing up that your grandmother
took you

**LocWoman:** Ah . I don't mind
I'm 55 and I was born in 194'6.
And we made this pilgrimage
Until she passed away in the early 60s.

**Edgar:** All right
So so you're talking nearly 200 years later
The feelings are still there among . the Scotch Irish
here in the
Backcountry.

(Edgar turns and calls on another audience member)
(Edgar and Swager 2002)

These comments follow a presentation by a University of South Carolina historian in which he discussed and, at times, read from his book, published by an academic press and validated by his professional credentials and ethics. The other participants contributed comments that helped focus discussion on the Revolutionary War role of the upland South Carolina area surrounding the battlefield.

Earlier in his speech, Dr. Edgar mentioned "Scotch Irish" several times and included material on the local Scotch Irish who were newly immigrated patriots to the countryside surrounding the battlefield just before the Revolutionary War. Audience comments, including those in the preceding example, indicate that most of those attending are descendants of these Scotch Irish settlers. Consequently, Edgar's lecture addresses topics pertinent to their family histories in a setting that evokes memories of legends, lore, and legacies of their ancestors.

In addition, the national park center setting, the National Park Service uniforms of the co-presenters, the white and local composition of the audience, and the Revolutionary War theme of the event invite participants to link the deeds of their white ancestors and their relationship to them to the formative documents and institutions of the United States (e.g., the Declaration of Independence and the Constitution). These entailments in turn situate the audience as members of a privileged group of white Americans who have the right by birth and by ancestors' deeds to employ, to claim, and to use core symbols of American political economy. This right centers them in the hegemonic historicism of whiteness in the upper American South rather than marginalizing them.

This woman audience member whose speech is captured in the C-SPAN transcript makes clear these processes of linkage to white "Americanness." She inserts a description of a family custom into the discussion in which "Scotch Irish" is discursive index (a nominal modifier) to a surname ("Carter"), which, in turn, indexically entails remembered conversations on "Scotch Irish" and "Carters" among members of this local audience. These comments also link her narrative to the historian's presentation through co-reference to Edgar's usage of "Scotch Irish" earlier. Kinship and genealogical references to her great-grandmother introduce links to genealogical discourse that would trace ancestry to a white Ulster, Northern Ireland, homeland. The stone-throwing narrative and Ulster-sympathetic reference to the English Revolutionary War officer and Kings Mountain casualty, Major Ferguson, as a "dirty rotten scoundrel" further validates her and her family's "rights" to be a white American whose ancestors were indisputable members of those who "founded" the United States as an independent nation.

Furthermore, the women's mastery of a folk narrative genre, that of the alleged historical origins of a contemporary phenomenon (a pile of stones on a grave), an origin tale as it were, neither contests nor questions the historical points made by the academic scholar. Instead, it augments the information by seemingly clarifying a historical point. Consequently, the text functions as a syncretization of oral family lore with established, and white, elitist scholarly discursive practices. The thematic structuring of a stone-throwing narrative may also exhibit similarity to an Ulster Irish narrative custom, thus providing interesting intercultural connections. Yet the pragmatics and metapragmatics indexed by this narrative do not contest the woman's participant role as an authentic voice for her family's privileged white American status as Scotch Irish, nor do they undercut each other by evoking different discursive representations of privilege, power, or rights of access. This verbal interaction does not exhibit the polyvocality or hybridization of the Melungeon Heritage Association's written text. Rather, it reproduces a well-honed, "traditionalized" (Bauman 1992) monovocal discursive valuation of "Scotch Irish" that reassures investors that this "object of value" will not be reappropriated or redistributed to those who cannot share in the use-rights to it.

With respect to issues of constructing "whiteness," then, these two examples reveal very different pragmatic and metapragmatic interconnections, leading to different ideologies of racial language. The text from the Melungeon Heritage Association's Web site presents a hybridization of elite and empowering discursive practices in which ethnonyms can circulate. These practices, however, are seemingly in conflict with each other in terms of their ideological functions and empowering purposes. One, that of validating "Melungeon" through inclusion in academic discourse, fails to entail the necessary conventional or expected discursive practices of validated scholarship. A second, of evoking a sense of sacred legitimization indexed by religious catechisms or tracts, is also weakly linked to other sacred texts through the absence of overt religious language. In addition, these two modes of authorization and empowerment, one by linguistic processes indexing scholarly achievement and accreditation, the other by linguistic signs indexing cosmological rights and divine approval, are, at a more abstract level, dichotomous sources of authority, one human, one divine.

Nevertheless, the impact of this text, and other texts offered in similar conventional modes, has been significant, at least in the Melungeon homeland centers and peripheries. This text and others similar to it in form and purpose are, indeed, hybrids, but hybrids in Swedenburg's formulation as forms that "often subversively appropriate and creolize master codes, decentering, destabilizing, and carnivalizing dominant forms through 'strategic inflections' and 'reaccentuations'" (Lavie and Swedenburg 1996:9). It is not that this text and other spoken and written authorizing texts for the Melungeon movement are changing whiteness necessarily, but they are creating opportunities for destabilization, for contesting "whiteness" in ways that may or may not effect change. Given the responses of the academy so far, they may only create boundaries, boundaries in which Melungeons remain marginalized or trivialized.

In the case of the second example, however, the ethnonym "Scotch Irish" presupposes and links folk narrative to white discursive practices of high value, the academic discussion. In so doing, it authorizes and substantiates symbols of white American political ideology. Rather than decentering whiteness, it centers it. Rather than destabilizing it, it anchors it in descent, place, family, and processes of shaping a particular and selective American history—all of which are white.

How these discursive practices interconnect, how they reproduce whiteness in seemingly "natural" ways or contest it in seemingly inauthentic arguments, must be more fully known, but known from the perspective of how discursive processes of valuation infuse ethnonyms for "racial" groups with rights of access, empowerment, and privilege. Then we can more fully understand the political-economic relations between the micro levels of verbal forms and the macro-level impacts of linguistic ideologies on how linguistic ideologies create or reproduce race relations. Without such insights, cultures of racism may not otherwise be changed.

## NOTES

I would like to thank the members of the Melungeon Heritage Association and other self-acknowledged Melungeons for sharing their thoughts and time with me. To the members of the communities who have allowed me to spend time with them, I also owe thanks, although I cannot name you by name. I would also like to thank Margaret Bender for her organizing the Southern Anthropological Association panel where this paper was first presented, for her thoughtful review and editorial comments, and for her diligence in editing this volume.

1. The full text is available at http://www.geocities.com/melungeonheritage/faq.html, accessed 29 July 2003.

2. Notes on transcription: Speech is transcribed as lines to capture intonational contours. Period indicates a short pause of .5 seconds. Square brackets, [ ], indicate overlapping verbalizations. Parentheses, ( ), describe gestural, paralinguistic, or other contextual cues. A stress mark, ', indicates increased stress on the following syllable.

## REFERENCES

*All Things Considered.* 1997. Melungeons. Washington, D.C.: National Public Radio.

Bauman, Richard. 1992. Contextualization, Tradition, and the Dialogue of Genres: Icelandic Legends of the *Kraftaskáld.* In *Rethinking Context: Language as an Interactive Phenomenon,* ed. Alessandro Duranti and Charles Goodwin, pp. 125–45. Cambridge: Cambridge University Press.

Bourdieu, Pierre. 1984. *Distinction: A Social Critique of the Judgment of Taste.* Trans. Richard Nice. Cambridge, Mass.: Harvard University Press.

Bucholtz, Mary. 2001. The Whiteness of Nerds: Superstandard English and Racial Markedness. *Journal of Linguistic Anthropology* 11:84–100.

Bucholtz, Mary, and Sara Trechter, eds. 2002. *Discourses of Whiteness. Journal of Linguistic Anthropology* 11 (special issue).

Duranti, Allesandro. 1997. *Linguistic Anthropology.* Cambridge Textbooks in Linguistics. Cambridge: Cambridge University Press.

Edgar, Walter, and Christine Swager. 2002. Speech: *Partisans and Redcoats*. Cowpens National Battlefield, Chesnee, South Carolina. C-SPAN Archives. West Lafayette, Indiana: National Cable Satellite Corporation.

Everett, Chris. 1999. Melungeon History and Myth. *Appalachian Journal* 26: 358–409.

Goffman, Irving. 1981. *Forms of Talk*. Philadelphia: University of Pennsylvania Press.

Graeber, David. 2001. *Toward an Anthropological Theory of Value: The False Coin of Our Own Dreams*. New York: Palgrave.

Henige David. 1998. Brent Kennedy's *Melungeon:* The Melungeons Become a Race. *Appalachian Journal* 25:270–86.

Hill, Jane. 1995. Junk Spanish, Covert Racism, and the (Leaky) Boundary between Public and Private Spheres. *Pragmatics* 5:197–212.

———. 2000. "Read My Article": Ideological Complexity and the Overdetermination of Promising in American Presidential Politics. In *Regimes of Language: Ideologies, Politics, and Identities,* ed. Paul V. Kroskrity, pp. 259–91. Santa Fe, N.M.: School of American Research.

———. 2001. Comments, Questions, and Enthusiastic Praise. *Journal of Linguistic Anthropology* 11:79–83.

Hymes, Dell. 1972. Models of the Interaction of Language and Social Life. In *Directions in Sociolinguistics: The Ethnography of Communication,* ed. John Gumperz and Dell Hymes, pp. 35–71. New York: Holt, Rinehart, and Winston.

Irvine, Judith. 1996. Shadow Conversations: The Indeterminacy of Participant Roles. In *Natural Histories of Discourse,* ed. Michael Silverstein and Greg Urban, pp. 131–59. Chicago: University of Chicago Press.

Irvine, Judith, and Susan Gal. 2000. Language Ideology and Linguistic Differentiation. In *Regimes of Language: Ideologies, Politics, and Identities,* ed. Paul V. Kroskrity, pp. 35–83. Santa Fe, N.M.: School of American Research.

Kennedy, N. Brent. 1994. *The Melungeons: The Resurrection of a Proud People: An Untold Story of Ethnic Cleansing in America*. Macon, Ga.: Mercer University Press.

Lavie, Smadar, and Ted Swedenburg. 1996. Introduction: Displacement, Diaspora, and Geographies of Identity. In *Displacment, Diaspora, and Geographies of Identity,* ed. Smadar Lavie and Ted Swedenburg, pp. 1–25. Durham, N.C.: Duke University Press.

Martin, Ernie, producer. 1997. *The Melungeons*. Kentucky Life 416. Lexington: Kentucky Educational Television.

Melungeon Heritage Association. http://www.geocities.com/melungeonheritage/faq.html, accessed 29 July 2003.

Montgomery, Michael. 2002. Eighteenth-Century Nomenclature for Ulster Emigrants. Paper presented at the Ulster American Heritage Symposium, Rock Hill, S.C.

Parmentier, Richard J. 1985. Times of the Signs: Modalities of History and Levels of Social Structure in Belau. In *Semiotic Mediation: Sociocultural and Psychological Perspectives,* ed. Elizabeth Mertz and Richard J. Parmentier, pp. 131–54. Orlando, Fla.: Academic Press.

Puckett, Anita. 2000. *Seldom Ask, Never Tell: Labor and Discourse in Appalachia.* Oxford Studies in Anthropological Linguistics. New York: Oxford University Press.

——— . 2001. The Melungeon Identity Movement and the Construction of Appalachian Whiteness. *Journal of Linguistic Anthropology* 11:131–46.

Scotch-Irish Society of the United States of America. http://www.rootsweb.com/~sisusa, accessed July 2002.

Silverstein, Michael. 1979. Language Structure and Linguistic Ideology. In *The Elements: A Parasession on Linguistic Units and Levels,* ed. P. R. Clyne, William Hanks, and C. Hofbauer, pp. 193–247. Chicago: Chicago Linguistic Society.

——— . 1984. The "Value" of Objectual Language. Paper presented at a symposium of the American Anthropology Association Meetings, Denver, Colo.

——— . 1993. Metapragmatic Discourse and Metapragmatic Function. In *Reflexive Language: Reported Speech and Metapragmatics,* ed. John Lucy, pp. 35–38. Cambridge: Cambridge University Press.

——— . 1996. Indexical Order and the Dialectics of Sociolinguistic Life. In *Symposium about Language and Society: Austin III,* ed. Risako Ide, Rebecca Parker, and Yukako Sunaoshi, pp. 266–95. Austin: Texas Linguistic Forum.

——— . 2001 [1981]. The Limits of Awareness. In *Linguistic Anthropology: A Reader,* ed. Alessandro Duranti, pp. 382–401. Malden, Mass.: Blackwell.

Sovine, Melanie. 1983. *The Mysterious Melungeon: A Critique of the Mythical Image*. Ph.D. dissertation, University of Kentucky, Lexington.

Urban, Gregory P. 1981. The Semiotics of Tabooed Food: The Shokleng Case. *Social Science Information* 20:475–507.

Winkler, Wayne, producer. 1999. *The Melungeons: Sons and Daughters of the Legend*. Radio documentary. Johnson City, Tenn.: WETS-FM.

# Contributors

MARGARET BENDER is an assistant professor of anthropology at Wake Forest University. She teaches courses in linguistic and cultural anthropology, gender studies, Native American studies, the anthropology of education, and anthropological theory. Her research has focused on the relationship between language and culture in a variety of contexts, from Cherokee medicinal practice to family literacy education in Chicago. Her recent book, *Signs of Cherokee Culture: Sequoyah's Syllabary in Eastern Cherokee Life* (2002, University of North Carolina Press), explores contemporary literacy practices among the Eastern Band of Cherokee Indians.

ELLEN FLUHARTY is a master's student in linguistics at West Virginia University. Her research interests include language variation and identity in midland Appalachia and dialect acquisition among homeschooled children. She plans to pursue a Ph.D.

LOUISE GOPHER graduated from Florida Atlantic University with a major in business. She was appointed Assistant Director of Education for the Seminole Tribe of Florida in 2002. She lives on the Brighton Reservation near Okeechobee, Florida, where she previously served as Education Counselor. She has served on the board of directors for the Florida Historical Society, the Ah-tah-thi-ki Museum, and the Florida Folk Life Council.

KIRK HAZEN is Woodburn Professor of Humanities for the Eberly College of Arts and Sciences at West Virginia University, where he directs the West Virginia Dialect Project. Some of his anthropologically oriented publications include "Identity and Language Variation in a Rural Community" (*Language* 78[2]), "The Role of Researcher Identity in Conducting Sociolinguistic Research" (*Southern Journal of Linguistics* 24[1]); "The Family" in *The Handbook of Language Variation and Change* (2001, Blackwell); and *Identity and Ethnicity in the Rural South* (2000, Duke University Press). Kirk is interested in both language variation research and improving teaching about language.

PAMELA INNES is an assistant professor in the Anthropology Department at the University of Wyoming. Her research interests are Native American languages and language revitalization issues. At present, she is working on developing language-teaching materials for use in college-level Mvskoke language courses.

CHRISTINE MALLINSON is a Ph.D. student in the Department of Sociology and Anthropology at North Carolina State University. Her interests are ethnicity, identity, and regional identity, and her research projects involve the intersection of these concepts with language and dialect. She coauthored an article with Walt Wolfram on the regional accommodation of African American English in Appalachia and is currently conducting fieldwork on a community of African Americans in Cherokee County, North Carolina. Her long-term research goal is to continue working with regional, social, and ethnic varieties of dialects and to continue investigating language as a marker of social identity.

BLAIR A. RUDES is an assistant professor of applied linguistics at the University of North Carolina at Charlotte. His work with speakers of the Tuscarora language over the past thirty years has resulted in the publication of two volumes of folklore (*The Tuscarora Legacy of J. N. B. Hewitt,* Canadian Museum of Civilization, 1987) and a bilingual dictionary (*Tuscarora-English/English-Tuscarora Dictionary,* University of Toronto Press, 1999). He is currently working with the Catawba Indian Nation to develop a grammar and dictionary of the Catawba language.

ANITA PUCKETT (Ph.D. Texas) is associate professor and director of the Appalachian Studies Program of the Center for Interdisciplinary Studies at Virginia Tech. She specializes in language and material relationships in southern Appalachia. Her research interests include ways in which language in use constitutes local socioeconomies and how various discursive forms can function much like material objects. These interests have also led her to investigate language and Internet relationships. Her first book, *Seldom Ask, Never Tell: Labor and Discourse in Appalachia* (Oxford 2000) explored (non)requesting patterns and socioeconomic relationships in a rural eastern Kentucky community. She is currently further exploring the comparative values of the ethnonyms "Melungeon" and "Scotch-Irish." This research is linked to an administrative and research collaboration between Virginia Tech's Appalachian Studies Program and the University of Ulster, Northern Ireland.

SUSAN E. STANS is an assistant professor at Florida Gulf Coast University, where she divides her time between teaching anthropology at the university and assisting the Seminole Tribe of Florida with their educational endeavors. She conducts the K–5 summer school program, *Emahakv Vpelofv,* at the Brighton Reservation. In May 2001, the University Press of Florida published her book with Seminole elder Alice Snow, *Healing Plants: The Medicine of the Seminole Indians*. At the request of tribal language teachers, she established a nondegree certificate program in teaching Florida native languages such as Creek and Mikasuki. She received bachelor degrees from the University of Florida (political science) and the University of Central Florida (anthropology). Her M.A. and Ph.D. degrees in anthropology are from the University of Florida.

SHANA WALTON (Ph.D. in anthropology, Tulane University) is associate director of the Deep South Regional Humanities Center at Tulane University in New Orleans, Louisiana. Research interests include language and identity, performance speech, life narratives, and whiteness studies, with fieldwork focusing on the South in general and the New Orleans Jazz and Heritage Festival in particular.

WALT WOLFRAM is the William C. Friday Distinguished Professor at North Carolina State University, where he also directs the North Carolina Language and Life Project. He has pioneered research on social and ethnic dialects since the 1960s, authoring or coauthoring more than 15 books and 250 articles on social and ethnic dialects of American English. His current research involves historically and culturally isolated dialect communities in North Carolina and beyond. He is also vitally concerned with the application of sociolinguistic information to social and educational problems and the dissemination of knowledge about dialects to the public. In this connection, he has been involved in the production of television documentaries on dialect diversity, the construction of museum exhibits, and the development of dialect awareness curricula for the schools. Wolfram is past president of the Linguistic Society of America and the American Dialect Society.